Editor
Sara Connolly

Cover Artist
Brenda DiAntonis

Editor in Chief
Ina Massler Levin, M.A.

Creative Director
Karen J. Goldfluss, M.S. Ed.

Imaging
James Edward Grace
Craig Gunnell

Publisher
Mary D. Smith, M.S. Ed.

COMPUTER PROJECTS

Grades 2-4

Includes Standards & Benchmarks

Integrate technology into the curriculum!

⭐ Computer lessons for Word Processing, Spreadsheets, and Presentations

⭐ Step-by-step instructions and screenshots

⭐ Works with a variety of software packages

Author

Steve Butz

Teacher Created Resources, Inc.
6421 Industry Way
Westminster, CA 92683
www.teachercreated.com

ISBN: 978-1-4206-2393-2

©2010 Teacher Created Resources, Inc.
Reprinted, 2014
Made in U.S.A.

Teacher Created Resources

Table of Contents

Word Processing Activities

Spreadsheet Activities

Presentation Activities

Introduction

Computer Activities for Grades 2–4 is an activity book that was created to accommodate teachers who would like to utilize computer technology to enhance their elementary school curriculum. The activities in this book were designed for use in a computer lab setting for grades two through four.

The book is arranged into three sections, which correlate to the use of three different types of software applications: word processing, spreadsheets, and presentations. There are twenty activities contained in this book that address the many different ways in which elementary educators can use software. This offers teachers the opportunity to confidently take classes into the computer lab and present a well-rounded lesson using the software available in their schools.

Presentation   **Spreadsheet**   **Word Processing**

Each activity is noted as it pertains to the topic of study, and everything needed to implement each lesson effectively is contained within the lab. Each activity has been successfully used in the classroom, and is designed to be completed in one, forty-five minute computer lab session.

No knowledge of software applications is required to teach the activities contained in this book. Each lab provides you with the overall purpose of the lesson, Learning Objectives, materials required, and detailed step-by-step procedures, along with informative pictures that show you exactly what to do. Although each lesson contains specific subject matter, all labs in this book can be easily adapted to fit your specific lesson plans by using your own data. The labs are designed to illustrate the many ways that computers can be used in your classroom to reinforce your specific topic of study, and then provide you with a variety of ways to incorporate technology into your curriculum.

Geometric Shapes
Activity 1

Objectives

Each student will utilize a word processing program to create a diagram that shows the following eleven basic geometric figures: square, triangle, rectangle, circle, parallelogram, hexagon, trapezoid, octagon, diamond, cube, and cylinder.

Benchmarks for Technology Standards

Students will know the characteristics, uses, and basic features of computer software programs, including:

- opening a file
- using basic menu commands and toolbar functions
- formatting text by centering lines
- using a word processor to apply formatting to text

Learning Objectives

At the end of this lesson, students will be able to:

1. Center, make bold, and underline the heading of a word processing document.
2. Draw eleven basic geometric shapes of various sizes using the Shapes tool.
3. Change the fill and line color of each geometric shape.
4. Use the Text Box tool to label each geometric figure.
5. Change the font size and alignment within a text box.

Before the Computer

This activity can be completed using most versions of Microsoft Word, Open Office, and iWorks.

Variations

Depending on the grade level and time allotted for this activity, you may choose to have your students create only the geometric figures without labeling them. If time and ability level allow, you may then choose to change the color of the shapes, and then label them as well. An example of a completed project is shown in Figure 1-1.

Geometric Shapes (cont.)
Activity 1

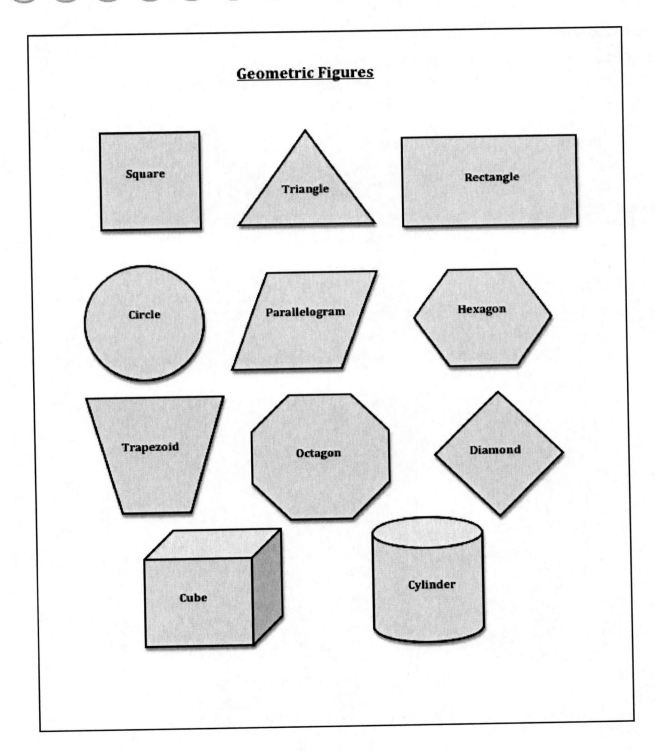

Figure 1-1

Geometric Shapes *(cont.)*
Activity 1

Procedure

1. Open a new word processing document.

2. Type the following heading at the top of the page: "Geometric Figures."

3. Highlight the heading by clicking and dragging over it.

4. Click on the **Align Center** button from the formatting toolbar. This should center your heading (see Figure 1-2).

Figure 1-2

5. Now click the **Bold** button (**B**) and **Underline** (U) buttons on the formatting toolbar. This will underline your heading and make it bold.

6. Next, display the **Drawing** toolbar by selecting the **View** menu, **Toolbars**, and **Drawing**.

7. On the Drawing toolbar, select the **AutoShapes**, **Shapes**, or **Basic Shapes** button (Figure 1-3).

Figure 1-3

Geometric Shapes *(cont.)*
Activity 1

8. Now click the **Square** icon and drag your cursor to the top-left portion of your document. Hold down the **shift** key as you click and drag to draw your square. (Holding down the shift key will ensure that your figure will be a perfect square and not a rectangle.) Make sure that your square is not too big (Figure 1-4).

Figure 1-4

9. Now that you have drawn your first geometric figure, you will change its color and add a label. If you are using Microsoft Word, double-click on the square to bring up the **Format AutoShapes** window. Change the **Fill** color for your square and click **OK**.

10. Now you will label your shape. To do this, click on the **Text Box** icon (Figure 1-5).

Figure 1-5

11. Drag your cursor to the middle of your square, and then click and draw a rectangle. You can now type in the label "Square." If you cannot read your text, click on one of the corners of the text box and drag it to make it larger (Figure 1-6).

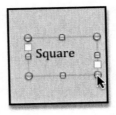

Figure 1-6

12. Repeat steps 7 through 12 to draw, color, and label the following geometric shapes: triangle, rectangle, circle, parallelogram, hexagon, trapezoid, octagon, diamond, cube, and cylinder.

Earth's Oceans and Continents Map
Activity 2

Objectives

Each student will utilize a word processing program to create and label a map of the world's oceans and continents.

Benchmarks for Technology Standards

Students will know the characteristics, uses, and basic features of computer software programs, including:

- the common features and uses of desktop publishing and word processing software
- knowing that documents can be created, designed, and formatted
- importing images into a document

Learning Objectives

At the end of this lesson, students will be able to:

1. Navigate to a website to access free, downloadable images.
2. Change the page layout for a document.
3. Import an image into a document.
4. Format an imported image.
5. Label an image using the text box tool.
6. Change the fill and line color of a text box.
7. Change the color and font of text within a text box.
8. Cite a reference for an image downloaded from a website.

Before the Computer

- This activity can be completed using most versions of Microsoft Word, Open Office, and iWorks.
- The following website is a great source for free, downloadable maps:
  http://www.worldatlas.com
  Check to make sure the website is available before teaching this lesson.

Variations

Depending on the grade level and time allotted for this activity, you may choose to have your students label their maps with only the names of each ocean or the continents. Also, if you have more experienced students and more time, they may be able to change the labels' font and color. An example of a completed project is shown in Figure 2-1.

Earth's Oceans & Continents Map (cont.)
Activity 2

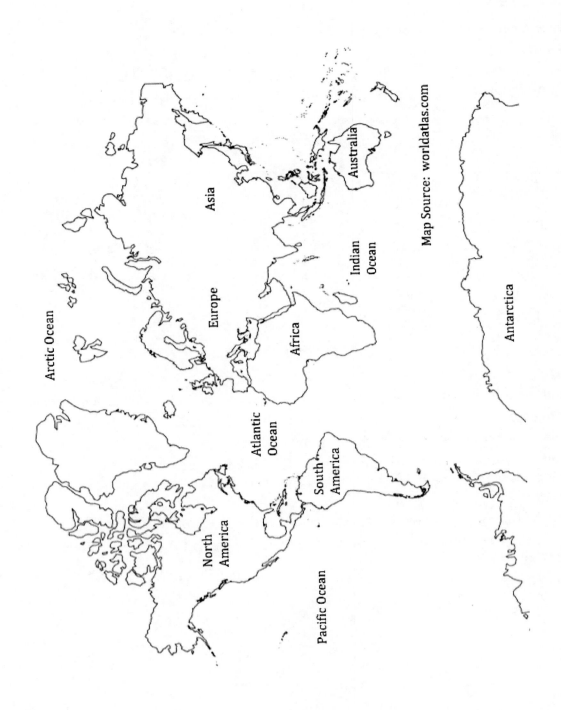

Figure 2-1

Earth's Oceans & Continents Map *(cont.)*
Activity 2

Procedure

1. Open a new word processing document.

2. If you are using Microsoft Word or Open Office, open the **View** menu and select **Print View**.

3. From the **File** menu, select **Page Setup**, and choose **Landscape** orientation (Figure 2-2). If you are using **Open Office**, choose the **Format** menu, and select **Page**.

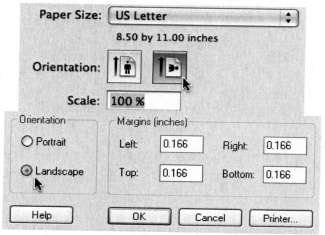

Figure 2-2

4. Next, using your web browser, navigate to the following website: **http://www.worldatlas.com**. Enter the website, scroll down, and click on the link on the right side labeled **Outline Maps**.

5. From the list, choose the **World (mercator no borders)** map.

6. Right-click (or control-click if you are using a Mac) on the map and choose **Copy**.

7. Return to your word processing document, and choose **Paste** from the **Edit** menu. You can also right-click (or control-click) on your page and choose **Paste**. The map should now be part of your document.

8. Next, you are going to label each continent using the **Text Box** tool.

9. If your drawing toolbar is not showing, select the **View** menu and choose **Toolbars**, then **Drawing**.

10. Select the **Text Box** tool (Figure 2-3).

Figure 2-3

Earth's Oceans & Continents Map *(cont.)*
Activity 2

11. Click and drag the **Text Box** tool over North America to make a large box (Figure 2-4).

Figure 2-4

12. Click inside of the text box you just drew and type the label "North America."

13. If you need to enlarge the text box to make the label fit, or move the text box, click on the box and then click and drag one of the anchor points on the corners to make the box smaller or larger. You can also move the text box by clicking on a line and dragging the entire box to a new location (Figure 2-5).

Figure 2-5

14. Continue labeling your map with the names of each continent and ocean.

15. Once your map is complete, insert a text box near the lower right side with the following reference: "Map Source: worldatlas.com" (Figure 2-6). Your map is now complete!

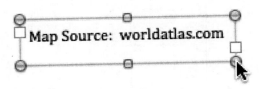

Figure 2-6

Math Tally Table
Activity 3

Objectives

Each student will create a table in a word processing document to use for a math tallying assignment.

Benchmarks for Technology Standards

Students will know the characteristics, uses, and basic features of computer software programs, including:

- the common features and uses of desktop publishing and word processing software
- knowing that documents can be created, designed, and formatted
- using a word processor to print text

Learning Objectives

At the end of this lesson, students will be able to:

1. Create a new word processing document.
2. Design and insert a table into a document.
3. Format a table.
4. Format the fill color of cells in a table.
5. Enter text into a table.
6. Format text within a table.

Before the Computer

This activity can be completed using most versions of Microsoft Word, Open Office, and iWorks.

Variations

Depending on the grade level and topic of study, you may choose to have students create a table to use to tally another set of data besides students' pets. An example of a completed document is shown in Figure 3-1.

Class Pets Tally Table

Pet	Tally
Dog	
Cat	
Bird	
Rodent	
Fish	
Rabbit	
Other	
None	

Figure 3-1

Math Tally Table *(cont.)*
Activity 3

Procedure

1. Open a new word processing document.

2. Type in the following title: "Class Pets Tally Table" and hit the **enter** key twice.

3. Highlight the title by clicking and dragging over it. Then center it by clicking on the **Align Center** icon (Figure 3-2). Your title should now be centered.

Figure 3-2

4. Increase the font size of your title by choosing the **Font Size** button and selecting **24** (Figure 3-3).

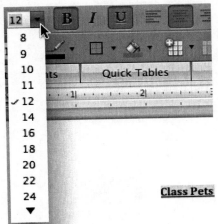

Figure 3-3

5. Select **Underline** and **Bold** buttons while your title is still highlighted (Figure 3-4).

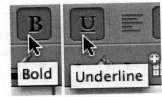

Figure 3-4

6. Use the **down arrow** key to move down two lines.

7. From the **Table** menu, choose **Insert** and **Table**. If you are using iWorks, click on the **table** icon.

8. In the **Insert Table** window, enter **2** for the number of columns, and **9** for the number of rows. Press **enter** and the table will appear in your document.

Math Tally Table *(cont.)*
Activity 3

9. Next, enter the following headings in the top two cells of your table: "Pet," "Tally."

10. Highlight your column headings in the first row of the table by clicking and dragging over them.

11. Click on the **Align Center** button to center your headings, then click on the **Font Size** button and change the font size to **24**.

12. Now fill in the type of pets in the first row of the first column (Figure 3-5).

Pet	Tally
Dog	
Cat	
Bird	
Rodent	
Fish	
Rabbit	
Other	
None	

Figure 3-5

13. Next, highlight the pet types by clicking and dragging over them. Change the size of the font to **22**.

14. Finally, you will change the shade of the headings within your table. To do this, highlight the headings and choose the **Cell Background Fill** tool from the table toolbar. Choose a light gray color (Figure 3-6).

Figure 3-6

15. Your table should now be complete and ready for printing (Figure 3-7).

Class Pets Tally Table

Pet	Tally
Dog	
Cat	
Bird	
Rodent	
Fish	
Rabbit	
Other	
None	

Figure 3-7

Spelling List
Activity 4

Objectives

Each student will create a word processing document containing a list of his or her current spelling words. They will then format the list into two columns and highlight the vowels within each word.

Benchmarks for Technology Standards

Students will know the characteristics, uses, and basic features of computer software programs, including:

- the common features and uses of desktop publishing and word processing software
- knowing the appropriate software for creating documents and that documents can be created, designed, and formatted
- using a word processing program to edit, center, and print text

Learning Objectives

At the end of this lesson, students will be able to:

1. Create a new word processing document.

2. Enter text into a document.

3. Format font size and style.

4. Divide a document into two columns.

5. Use keyboard commands to format text.

6. Add a header to a document.

Before the Computer

This activity can be completed using most versions of Microsoft Word, Open Office, and iWorks.

Variations

This activity works best when your students use their current spelling words. The words contained in this activity are used only to provide an example of how to perform this lab. Using twenty spelling words works very well for this activity. You may wish to lengthen or shorten the number of spelling words for their lists, according to the time you are allotting for this activity and the ability level of your students. An example of a completed document is shown in Figure 4-1.

Spelling List *(cont.)*
Activity 4

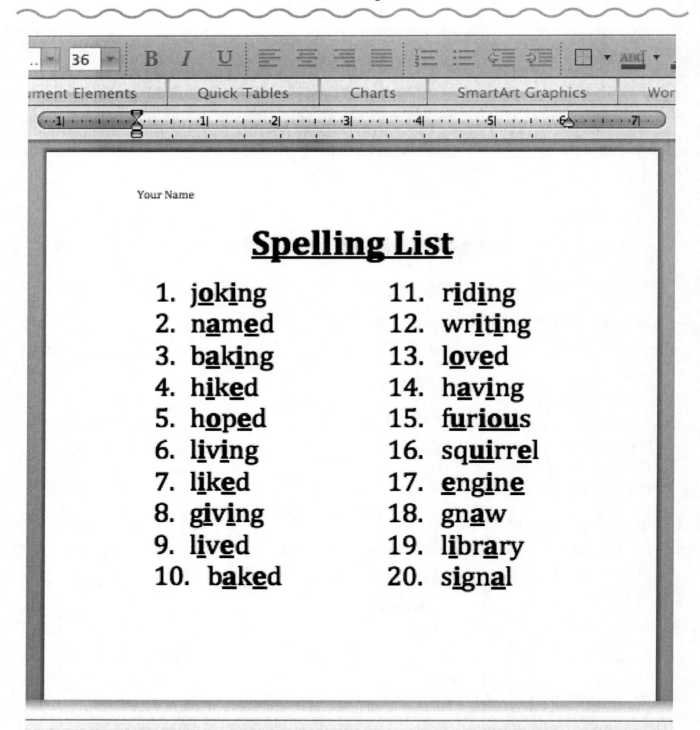

Your Name

Spelling List

1. joking
2. named
3. baking
4. hiked
5. hoped
6. living
7. liked
8. giving
9. lived
10. baked

11. riding
12. writing
13. loved
14. having
15. furious
16. squirrel
17. engine
18. gnaw
19. library
20. signal

Figure 4-1

Spelling List *(cont.)*
Activity 4

Procedure

1. Open a new word processing document.

2. At the top of the document type in the following title: "Spelling List."

3. Hit **enter** twice on your keyboard to bring your cursor two lines below your title, and type in the number **1**, then hit the **tab** key on your keyboard.

4. Type in your first spelling word, then hit **enter**. The number **2** should automatically appear below number 1. Type your next spelling word.

5. Continue until you have entered all of your spelling words.

6. Highlight your title by clicking and dragging over it.

7. Next, center your title by clicking the **Align Center** button (Figure 4-2), then underline and make it bold using the **Bold** and **Underline** buttons (Figure 4-3).

Figure 4-2

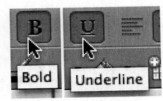

Figure 4-3

8. With your title still highlighted, increase its font size to **36** by clicking the **Font Size** tool (Figure 4-4).

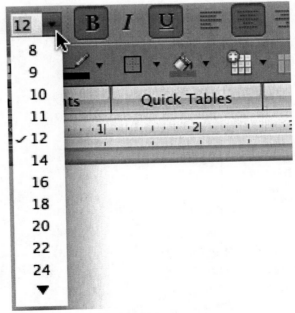

Figure 4-4

Spelling List *(cont.)*
Activity 4

9. Next, click and drag over all of your spelling words to highlight them. Then change their font size to **28**.

10. Now you are going to divide your spelling list into two columns. With your spelling list still highlighted, open the **Format** menu and choose **Columns** (Figure 4-5). If you are using iWorks, choose the **View** menu, select **Show Layout**, and choose the **Layout Inspector** (Figure 4-6).

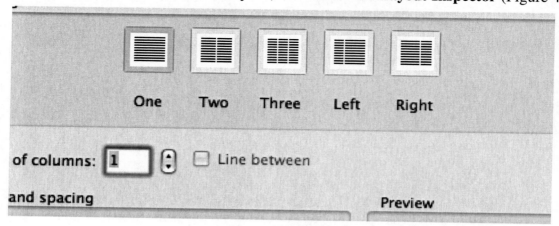

One   Two   Three   Left   Right

of columns: 1 ⬍ ☐ Line between

and spacing   Preview

Figure 4-5

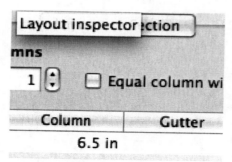

Layout inspector :ction

mns

1 ⬍ ☐ Equal column wi

Column	Gutter
6.5 in	

Figure 4-6

11. Change the number of columns from **One** to **Two**. Your spelling list should now be divided into two columns.

12. Highlight the vowels in each word, and make them bold and underlined by using the **Bold** and **Underline** buttons. You may also try to underline and make them bold by holding down the **control** key while hitting either the **B** key for bold or **U** key for underline. (If you are using a Mac, you must hold down the **command** key.)

13. Finally, you will add a header that holds your name. To do this in Microsoft Word, open the **View** menu and choose **Header and Footer**. If you are using iWorks, open the **View** menu and choose **Show Layout**. If you are using Open Office, open the **Insert** menu and choose **Header**. Then type in your first and last name.

14. Your spelling list is now ready to print.

Food Chain Diagram
Activity 5

Objectives

Each student will utilize a word processing program to create and label a diagram of a simple food chain.

Benchmarks for Technology Standards

Students will know the characteristics, uses, and basic features of computer software programs, including:

- the common features and uses of desktop publishing and word processing software
- knowing that documents can be created, designed, and formatted
- importing images into a document

Learning Objectives

At the end of this lesson, students will be able to:

1. Change the page layout for a document.

2. Center, make bold, and increase font size.

3. Navigate to a website to access free downloadable images.

4. Import an image into a document.

5. Format an imported image.

6. Label an image using the text box tool.

7. Draw arrows using the lines tool.

8. Cite a reference for an image downloaded from a website.

Before the Computer

- This activity can be completed using most versions of Microsoft Word, Open Office, and iWorks.
- The following websites are a great source for free, downloadable clip art images: **http://office.microsoft.com/en-us/clipart** or **http://classroomclipart.com**

  Check to make sure the website you choose to use for this activity is available, and you are able to copy and paste the clip art they contain into a document before teaching this lesson. Also, if you choose to use the Microsoft website, instruct your students to filter their searches only for clip art. This can be done by clicking the arrow on the **Search** button, and choosing **Clip art**.

Variations

Depending on the grade level and time allotted for this activity, you may choose to have your students create more than one food chain using other organisms or ecosystems, and also label each organism as a producer or consumer. An example of a completed project is shown in Figure 5-1.

Food Chain Diagram (cont.)
Activity 5

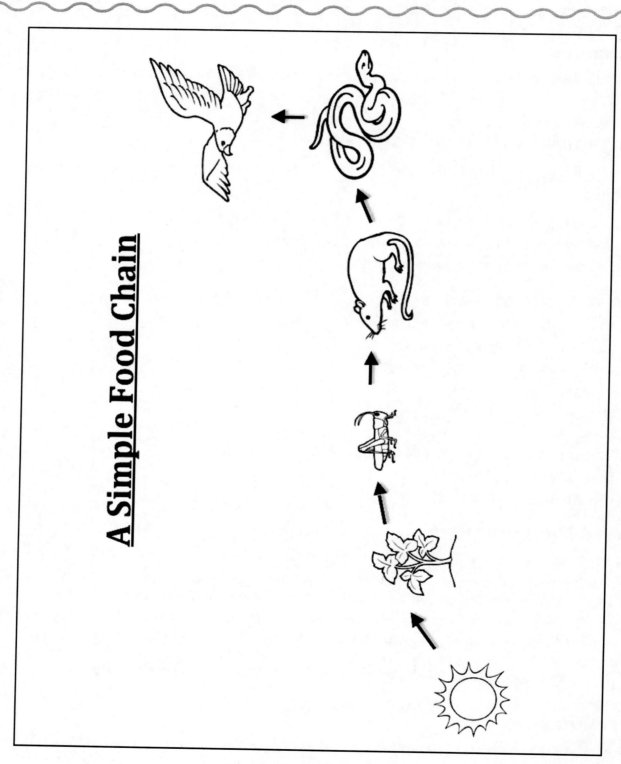

Figure 5-1

Food Chain Diagram *(cont.)*
Activity 5

Procedure

1. Open a new word processing document.

2. If you are using Microsoft Word or Open Office, open the **View** menu and select **Print View**.

3. From the **File** menu, select **Page Setup**, and choose **Landscape** orientation (Figure 5-2). If you are using Open Office, choose the **Format** menu, and **Page**.

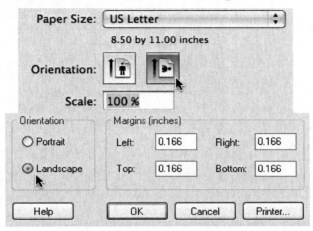

Figure 5-2

4. Next, type in the following title: "A Simple Food Chain."

5. Highlight your title by clicking and dragging over it. Then increase its font size to **36** by clicking the **Font Size** button.

6. With your title still highlighted, make it bold and underlined by using the **Bold** and **Underline** buttons (Figure 5-3). You may also try to underline it and make it bold by holding down the **control** key while hitting either the **B** key for bold or **U** key for underline. (If you are using a Mac, you must hold down the **command** key.) Click the **Align Center** button to center your title.

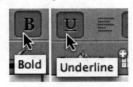

Figure 5-3

7. Next, open up your web browser and navigate to one of the following websites that your teacher has instructed you to go to:

http://office.microsoft.com/en-us/clipart or **http://classroomclipart.com**

8. These websites hold many free, downloadable images that can be imported into your word processing document. You are going to use one of them to access images of organisms that will make up your food chain. In the search box on the webpage, type in the word "Sun."

Food Chain Diagram *(cont.)*
Activity 5

9. Your search should reveal many different images representing the sun. Locate one you like, and click on the copy icon below the image (Figure 5-4), or right-click on your mouse (or control-click if you are using a Mac) and choose **Copy Image** (Figure 5-5).

Figure 5-4

| Open Link in New Window |
| Open Link in New Tab |
| |
| Bookmark This Link |
| Save Link As... |
| Send Link... |
| Copy Link Location |
| |
| View Image |
| **Copy Image** |

Figure 5-5

10. Return to your word processing document, and choose **Paste** from the **Edit** menu. You can also right-click on your document and choose **Paste**. The image should now be part of your document.

11. Next, you'll need to format the image so you can place it where you want in the document. To do this, double-click on the image to bring up the **Format Picture** window. Choose **Layout**, and **In Front of Text**. Now you can click and drag your sun image to the bottom left-hand corner of your page.

12. Now you will draw an arrow using the line tool to show the flow of energy from the sun to the next level of the food chain. To do this, go to the **View** menu, select **Toolbars**, and choose **Drawing**.

Food Chain Diagram (cont.)
Activity 5

13. Next, select the **Line** tool and **Arrow** (Figure 5-6, Figure 5-7).

Figure 5-6   **Figure 5-7**

14. Click and drag your mouse to draw a short arrow pointing from your sun (Figure 5-8).

Figure 5-8

15. Next, return to the clip art website and locate an image of a plant. Copy and paste it into your word processing document.

16. Double-click on the image to bring up the **Format Picture** window. Choose **Layout**, and **In Front of Text**. Now you can click and drag your plant image just to the upper right of the sun image and its arrow (Figure 5-9).

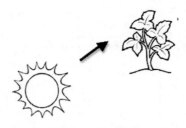

Figure 5-9

17. When you are finished with your food chain, select the **View** menu and **Header and Footer**. Then type in the website address you used for your images (Figure 5-10). Your food chain is now complete!

Image source: www.classroomclipart.com

Figure 5-10

United States Region Map
Activity 6

Objectives

Each student will utilize a word processing program to create and label a map of the continental United States, showing its four main geographic regions.

Benchmarks for Technology Standards

Students will know the characteristics, uses, and basic features of computer software programs, including:

- the common features and uses of desktop publishing and word processing software
- knowing that documents can be created, designed, and formatted
- importing images into a document

Learning Objectives

At the end of this lesson, students will be able to:

1. Navigate to a website to access free, downloadable images.
2. Change the page layout for a document.
3. Import an image into a document.
4. Format an imported image.
5. Label an image using the text box tool.
6. Alter the transparency of a background image.
7. Change the color and font of text within a text box.
8. Cite a reference for an image downloaded from a website.
9. Add a header and footer to a document.

Before the Computer

- This activity can be completed using most versions of Microsoft Word, Open Office and iWorks.
- The following website is a great source for free, downloadable maps:
  http://www.worldatlas.com
  Check to make sure the website is available before teaching this lesson.

Variations

Depending on the grade level and time allotted for this activity, you may choose to have your students change the region labels' font type and color. An example of a completed project is shown in Figure 6-1.

United States Region Map (cont.)
Activity 6

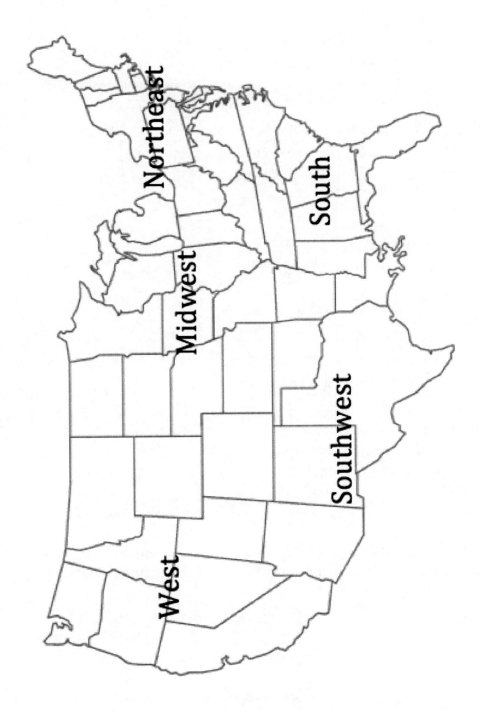

Regions of the Continental United States

Map Source: worldatlas.com

Figure 6-1

United States Region Map *(cont.)*
Activity 6

Procedure

1. Open a new word processing document.

2. If you are using Microsoft Word or Open Office, open the **View** menu and select **Print View**.

3. From the **File** menu, select **Page Setup**, and choose **Landscape** orientation (Figure 6-2). If you are using Open Office, choose the **Format** menu, and select **Page**.

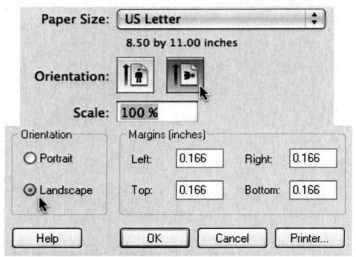

Figure 6-2

4. Next, using your web browser, navigate to the following website: **http://www.worldatlas.com**. Enter the website, scroll down, and click on the link on the right side labeled **Outline Maps**.

5. From the list choose the **USA (48 states)** map.

6. Right-click on the map (or control-click if you are using a Mac) and choose **Copy**.

7. Return to your word processing document, and choose **Paste** from the **Edit** menu. You can also right-click (or control-click) on your document and choose **Paste**. The map should now be part of your document.

8. Now you will resize your map so it fills the entire page. Go to the **View** menu, and choose **Zoom**. Reduce the size of the display of your document to 75%. You can also change the viewing size by using the **Zoom** tool on your toolbar (Figure 6-3).

Figure 6-3

United States Region Map *(cont.)*
Activity 6

9. Next, click on your map once to show the image's anchor points. Click and drag the bottom right corner of your map so it fills the entire page (Figure 6-4).

Figure 6-4

10. Right-click (or control-click) on the map, choose **Arrange**, and select **Behind Text**. This will then allow you to type labels on top of your map. If you are using Open Office, choose **Wrap**, then **No Wrap**.

11. Next, you will change the transparency of your map so your labels will be easier to read. Right click on your map, choose **Format Picture**, click the **Picture** button, and set the transparency to **50%** (Figure 6-5).

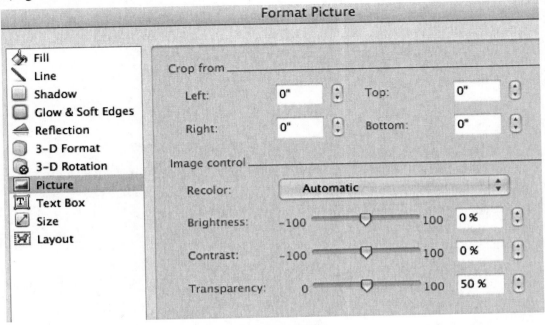

Figure 6-5

United States Region Map *(cont.)*
Activity 6

12. If your Drawing toolbar is not showing, select the **View** menu, choose **Toolbars**, then select **Drawing**.

13. Select the **Text Box** tool (Figure 6-6).

Figure 6-6

14. Next you are going to label each region of the United States. Click and drag the **Text Box** tool over the upper-right portion of your map to make a large box. Change the size of your font to **24**, and type "Northeast." (Figure 6-7).

Figure 6-7

15. Continue to add labels for each of the four remaining regions: "South," "Midwest," "West," and "Southwest" (Figure 6-1).

16. Once your map is complete, you will insert a header that will contain the map's title. From the **View** menu, choose **Header and Footer.** Type in the following: "Regions of the Continental United States." Center your title using the **Align Center** tool.

17. Next, you will cite the source where you downloaded your map image. Type the following text in the footer section of your document: "Map Source: www.worldatlas.com." If you are using Open Office, go to the **Insert** menu and choose **Header or Footer**.

18. Your map is now complete!

Cut-and-Paste Story Sequence
Activity 7

Objectives

Each student will utilize a word processing program to cut and paste sequences of a story in the correct order.

Benchmarks for Technology Standards

Students will know the characteristics, uses, and basic features of computer software programs, including:

- the common features and uses of desktop publishing and word processing software
- knowing that documents can be created, designed, and formatted

Learning Objectives

At the end of this lesson, students will be able to:

1. Open a new word processing document.

2. Enter and format text into a document.

3. Use the cut-and-paste functions to copy text from one document and paste it into another.

4. Create a numbered list.

Before the Computer

- This activity can be completed using most versions of Microsoft Word, Open Office, and iWorks.
- An example story sequence using "Bed in Summer" by Robert Louis Stevenson, is provided, but you may also choose to use your own longer or shorter story sequences from another book or poem your class is reading. An example of a completed project is shown in Figure 7-1.

Bed in Summer

By Robert Louis Stevenson

1. In Winter I get up at night
2. And dress by yellow candle light.
3. In Summer, quite the other way,
4. I have to go to bed by day.
5. I have to go to bed and see
6. The birds still hopping on the tree,
7. Or hear the grown-up people's feet
8. Still going past me in the street.

Figure 7-1

Cut and Paste Story Sequence *(cont.)*
Activity 7

Procedure

1. Begin this activity by reading the passages from your poem or story provided by your teacher, or in Figure 7-2.

Bed in Summer

By Robert Louis Stevenson

I have to go to bed by day.
The birds still hopping on the tree,
Still going past me in the street.
In Winter I get up at night

And dress by yellow candle light.
In Summer, quite the other way,
I have to go to bed and see
Or hear the grown-up people's feet

Figure 7-2

2. Next, open a new word processing document and type in the title of the story or poem and the author's name.

3. Highlight the text by clicking and dragging over it, then center it by using the **Align Center** button. Make the text bold, and increase its font size to **18** (Figure 7-3).

Figure 7-3

4. Next, you are going to type the sentences from your story or poem in the order provided into your document (Figure 7-2).

5. Once you have typed in all sentences, save your work, and then open up a new word processing document.

6. Type in the same title and author for your sequence, center the text, make it bold, and increase the font size to **18**.

Cut and Paste Story Sequence *(cont.)*
Activity 7

7. Return to the first document containing your sentences. Choose the sentence that you think is the first in the story sequence. Highlight it by clicking and dragging over it. Then choose the **Edit** menu, and **Cut**. You can also right-click on your highlighted text (or control-click if you are using a Mac) to choose the **Cut** function (Figure 7-4).

I have to go to bed by day.
The birds still hopping on the tree,
Still going past me in the street.
In Winter I get up at night

Help	
Cut	⌘X
Copy	⌘C
Paste	⌘V
Paste Special...	

And dress by yellow candle li
In Summer, quite the other w
I have to go to bed and se
Or hear the grown-up people'

Figure 7-4

8. Click into your document just below your title, and set the alignment by clicking the **Align Left** button. Now choose the **Edit** menu and **Paste** to insert your sentence. You can also right-click (or control-click) on your page, and choose **Paste**.

9. Click so your cursor is in front of the sentence you just pasted. Locate the **Numbering** button on the toolbar, and click on it. This will automatically create a numbered list for your sentences (Figure 7-5). The Number 1 should automatically appear.

Figure 7-5

10. Click to the end of your first sentence and hit the **enter** key. The number 2 should appear automatically.

11. Return to the other document, highlight the next sentence in the sequence, and then copy and paste it into the other document. Repeat until your story is complete! To turn off the Numbering function, just click the **Numbering** button again.

If I Were President
Activity 8

Objectives

Each student will create a word processing document containing four panels, illustrating what he or she would do if he or she were the President of the United States.

Benchmarks for Technology Standards

Students will know the characteristics, uses, and basic features of computer software programs, including:

- the common features and uses of desktop publishing and word processing software
- knowing the appropriate software for creating documents and that documents can be created, designed and formatted
- using a word processing program to edit, center, and print text

Learning Objectives

At the end of this lesson, students will be able to:

1. Create a new word processing document.
2. Enter text into a document.
3. Format font size and style.
4. Import a photo into a document.
5. Use the Callout tool.
6. Enter and format text within a callout.

Before the Computer

- This activity can be completed using most versions of Microsoft Word, Open Office, and iWorks.
- Prior to conducting this lesson, you will need to take a digital photograph of each student, and make the photos accessible at their computer workstation(s). Each student should also come prepared with four written statements about what he or she would do if he or she were President of the United States. You should also make sure the following website is accessible for the lesson:

http://www.usa-flag-site.org/images.shtml

Variations

Depending on the age and ability level of your students, you may wish to have students create more than four things they would do as President of the United States. An example of a completed document is shown in Figure 8-1.

If I Were President *(cont.)*
Activity 8

**If I Were President
By Nancy Tung**

I would help stop pollution and stop people from cutting down the rain forests.

I would help the environment and change prices so that you could afford things.

I would destroy all guns!

I would help lower gas prices.

Figure 8-1

If I Were President *(cont.)*
Activity 8

Procedure

1. Open a new word processing document.

2. If you are using Microsoft Word or Open Office, open the **View** menu and select **Print View**.

3. Type in the following title at the top of your document: "If I Were President."

4. Below your title, type "by (Your First Name) (Your Last Name)."

5. Click and drag over your name and the title to highlight them. Center your title using the **Align Center** tool, increase the font size to **18**, and change its style to **Bold** using the buttons on the toolbar (Figure 8-2).

Figure 8-2

6. Next you will import an image of yourself that was taken by your teacher earlier. Choose the **Insert** menu, **Picture**, then **From File**. Have your teacher help you navigate to the image file of you, and then insert it into your document.

7. Once your picture is imported, right-click on it (or control-click if you are using a Mac) and change the text wrapping to **Behind Text**. Move the image to the middle of your page. You may also have to re-size it by clicking and dragging one of the corner anchor points (Figure 8-3).

Figure 8-3

8. Next, open your web browser and navigate to the following website:

http://www.usa-flag-site.org/images.shtml

9. Right-click (or control-click) on the image of the flag on a stand, and choose **Copy Image**.

10. Paste the image into your document by going to the **Edit** menu and selecting **Paste**. You can also right-click (or control-click) on your page and choose **Paste**. The flag image should now be inserted into your document.

11. Right-click (or control-click) on the flag image and choose **Text Wrapping** and **Behind Text**. Click and drag your flag image to the left of your picture.

If I Were President *(cont.)*
Activity 8

12. Next, you will use the Callout Box tool. A callout box is often used in comics or other drawings as a way of showing what people are saying.

13. If your drawing toolbar is not visible, choose the **View** menu, **Toolbars**, and **Drawing**. On the drawing toolbar, click **AutoShapes** and **Callouts** (Figure 8-4).

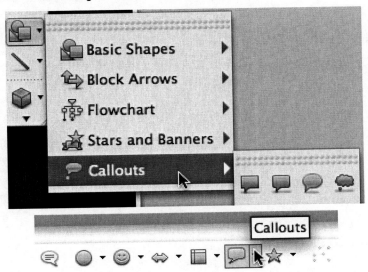

Figure 8-4

14. Choose a callout, and click and drag it near the upper right side of your document. Click inside the callout box, and type in your first statement about what you would do if you were President. After you are done typing, highlight the text and increase its font size so it fills up the box. Then center the text using the **Align Center** button. If you click on the callout box, you will see a yellow dot. You can click and drag the dot to align it near your mouth, so it looks like you are speaking (Figure 8-5).

Figure 8-5

15. Repeat the same process for inserting callout boxes for your three remaining statements. Your project is now complete!

Ecosystem Energy Pyramid
Activity 9

Objectives

Each student will create a word processing document illustrating a typical energy pyramid for an ecosystem.

Benchmarks for Technology Standards

Students will know the characteristics, uses, and basic features of computer software programs, including:

- the common features and uses of desktop publishing and word processing software
- knowing the appropriate software for creating documents and that documents can be created, designed, and formatted
- using a word processing program to edit, center, and print text
- using basic menu commands and toolbar functions
- formatting text by centering lines
- uses a word processor to apply formatting to text

Learning Objectives

At the end of this lesson, students will be able to:

1. Create a new word processing document.
2. Enter text into a document.
3. Format font size and style.
4. Draw geometric shapes of various sizes using the shapes tool.
5. Change the fill and line color of each geometric shape.
6. Use the text box tool to label each geometric figure.
7. Change the font size and alignment within a text box.

Before the Computer

This activity can be completed using most versions of Microsoft Word, Open Office, and iWorks.

Variations

Depending on the age and ability level of your students, you may wish to have students add energy values and units to their pyramid, illustrating the transfer and loss of energy from one level of the pyramid to another. An example of a completed document is shown in Figure 9-1.

Ecosystem Energy Pyramid *(cont.)*
Activity 9

Ecosystem Energy Pyramid

Fourth Trophic Level
Third-Level Consumer

Third Trophic Level
Secondary Consumer

Second Trophic Level
Primary Consumer

First Trophic Level
Producer

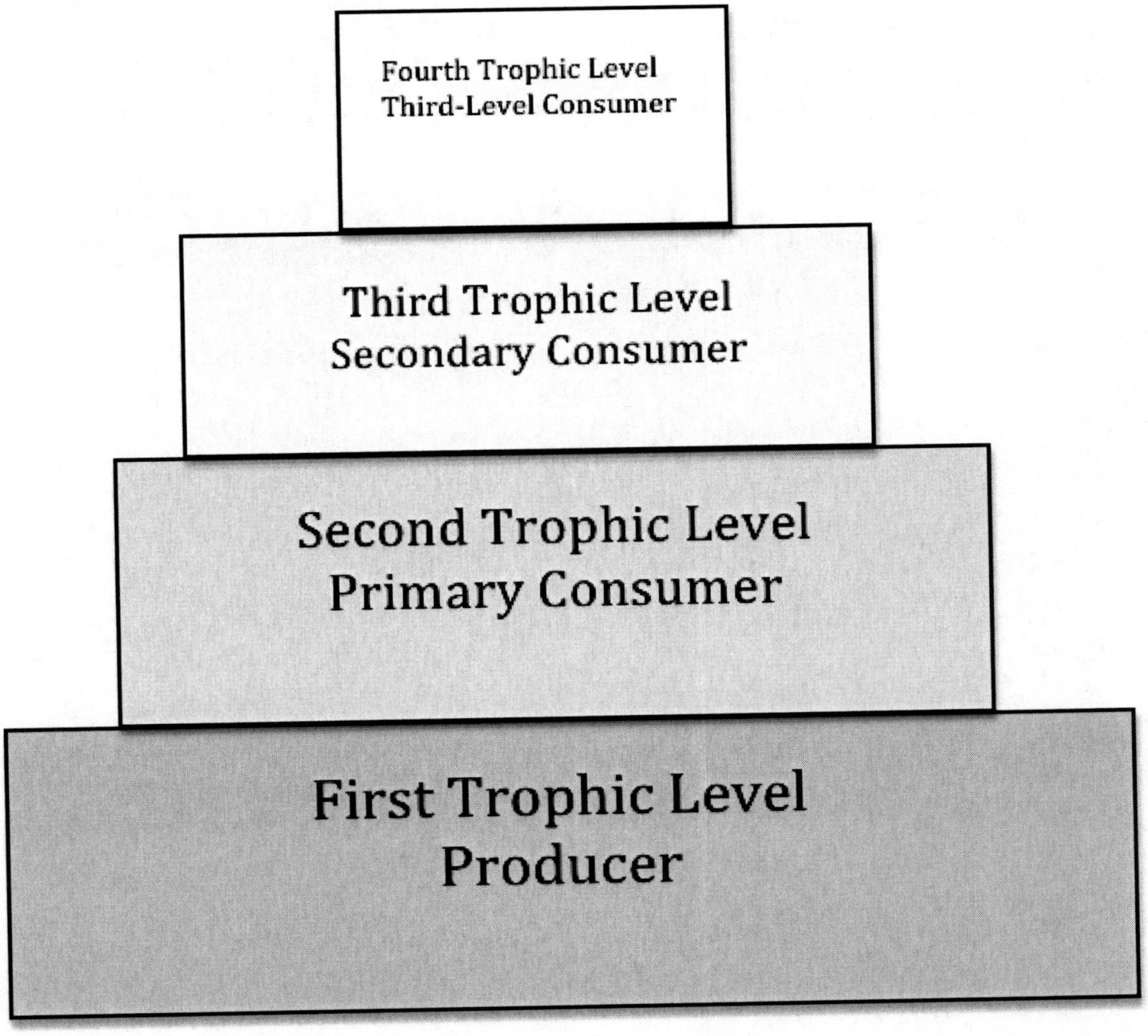

Figure 9-1

Ecosystem Energy Pyramid *(cont.)*
Activity 9

Procedure

1. Open a new word processing document.

2. If you are using Microsoft Word or Open Office, open the **View** menu and select **Print View**.

3. Type in the following title at the top of your document: "Ecosystem Energy Pyramid."

4. Click and drag over your name and the title to highlight them. Center your title using the **Align Center** tool, increase the font size to **18**, and change its style to **bold** using the buttons on the toolbar (Figure 9-2).

Figure 9-2

5. Next, display the Drawing toolbar by selecting the **View** menu, **Toolbars**, and **Drawing**.

6. On the **Drawing** toolbar, select the **AutoShapes**, **Shapes**, or **Basic Shapes** button, and choose the **Rectangle** (Figure 9-3).

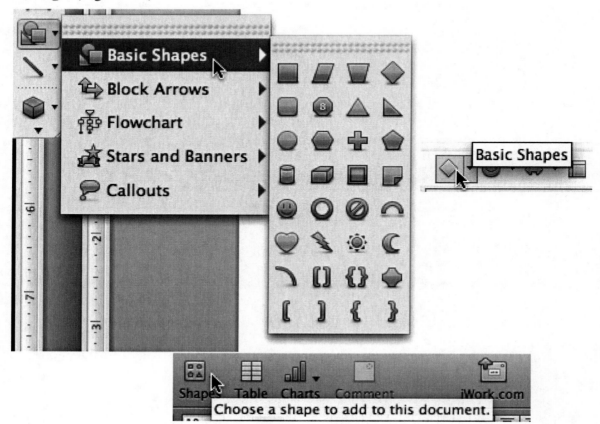

Figure 9-3

Ecosystem Energy Pyramid *(cont.)*
Activity 9

7. Click and drag your rectangle to stretch the width of your page near the bottom (Figure 9-4).

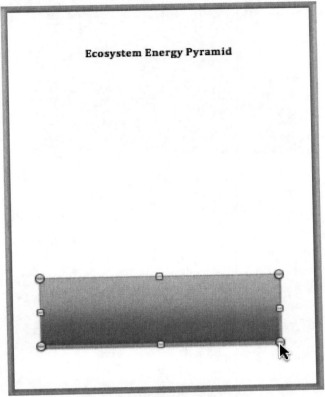

Figure 9-4

8. Double-click on your rectangle, and choose **Color and Lines**. Change the **Fill** color to a **50%** **gray**. If you are using **Open Office**, right-click (or control-click) on your rectangle and choose **Area** and **40% gray** (Figure 9-5).

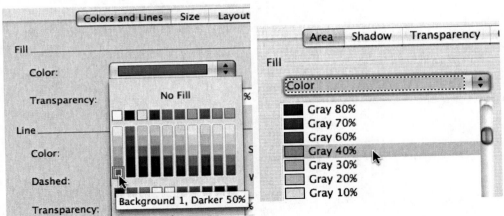

Figure 9-5

Ecosystem Energy Pyramid (cont.)
Activity 9

9. Next, draw another rectangle, a little less wide, on top of the first rectangle (Figure 9-6).

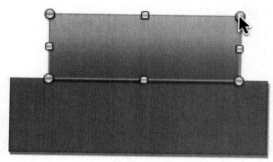

Figure 9-6

10. Change the fill color for the new rectangle using a shade of gray a little lighter than the first level of your energy pyramid.

11. Add two other rectangles, continuing to build your pyramid. Make sure each new level is a little less wide, and one shade of gray lighter than the one below it (Figure 9-7).

Figure 9-7

12. Now it is time to label the four levels of your energy pyramid. Click on the **Text Box** tool and use it to draw a rectangular box on top of your first energy level (Figure 9-8).

Figure 9-8

Ecosystem Energy Pyramid *(cont.)*
Activity 9

13. After you draw your text box, change the font size to **24**, and type in the following label:

First Trophic Level
Producer

14. Click and drag over your label and center it using the **Align Center** button on your tool bar (Figure 9-9).

Figure 9-9

15. Use the **Text Box** tool to add the following label to the next level of your pyramid. This time set the font size to **22**.

Second Trophic Level
Primary Consumer

16. Label the final two levels, using a font size of **18** for the third level, and **12** for the fourth (Figure 9-10).

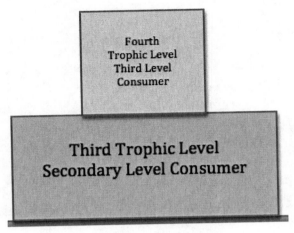

Figure 9-10

17. Your energy pyramid is now complete!

Money Math Bar Graph
Activity 10

Objectives

Each student will practice their money math skills and enter number data into a spreadsheet to create a simple bar graph.

Benchmarks for Technology Standards

Students will know the characteristics, uses, and basic features of computer software programs, including:

- knowing the common features and uses of spreadsheets
- using spreadsheet software to update, add, and delete data, and to produce charts

Learning Objectives

At the end of this lesson, students will be able to:

1. Identify the value of different coins.
2. Know the various terms associated with spreadsheets, including *rows*, *columns*, and *cells*.
3. Enter data into a spreadsheet.
4. Adjust the width of a selected column.
5. Change the alignment of data within a cell.
6. Change the style of data within a cell.
7. Create and format a bar chart from data entered within a spreadsheet.

Before the Computer

- This activity can be completed using most versions of Microsoft Excel, Open Office, and iWorks.
- The procedure for formatting charts using spreadsheets may vary depending on the software and version your school uses. Make sure to try the activity with your school's spreadsheet software, and be prepared to modify the chart procedure accordingly.

Variations

Depending on the age and ability level of your students, you may wish to have students use assignments in money math from class to create their spreadsheet and chart. An example of a completed bar graph is shown in Figure 10-1.

Money Math Bar Graph (cont.)
Activity 10

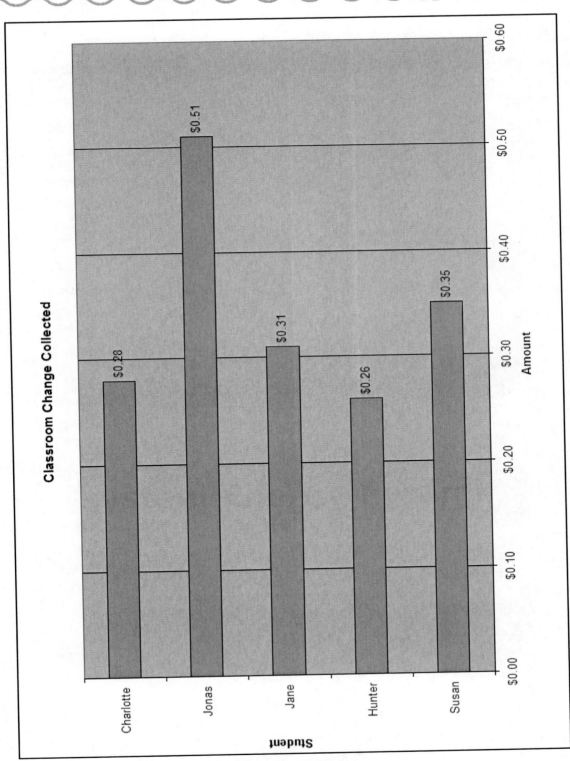

Figure 10-1

Money Math Bar Graph *(cont.)*
Activity 10

Procedure

1. Complete the money math problems representing the amount of money collected by six students, shown in Figure 10-2.

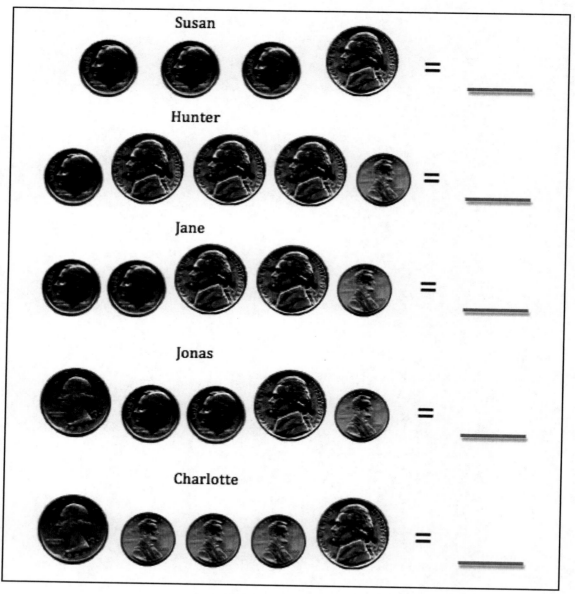

Figure 10-2

2. Open a new spreadsheet document. Spreadsheets are made up of columns that are identified by letters (A, B, C, etc.) and rows that are identified by numbers (1, 2, 3, etc.).

Money Math Bar Graph (cont.)
Activity 10

3. The location within a spreadsheet where a column meets a row is called a cell, and is identified by both a letter and number (Figure 10-3).

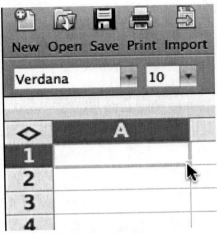

Figure 10-3

4. Click into cell **A1**, and type in the following label: "Student." Hit the **enter** key on your keyboard to bring you down to cell **A2**, and type in the name "Susan." Continue to fill each remaining student's name into Column A.

5. Next click into cell **B1** and type in the following label: "Change Collected." Hit the **enter** key on your keyboard and type in the value for the total money collected by each student. Enter the number as a decimal. For example, 25 cents would be entered as .25.

6. Next, click and drag over the two column labels, and use the **Bold** button on your toolbar (Figure 10-4).

	A	Change Collected
1	**Student**	**Change Collected**
2	Susan	0.35
3	Hunter	0.26
4	Jane	0.31
5	Jonas	0.51
6	Charlotte	0.28
7		

Figure 10-4

Money Math Bar Graph *(cont.)*
Activity 10

7. Next, you will have to widen column B so the label fits within it. To do this, take your cursor and place it on the line separating columns A and B. Then click and drag your cursor to the right until the cell is wide enough for the "Change Collected" label to fit in (Figure 10-5).

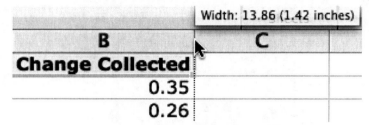

Figure 10-5

8. Now you will center your the data in your cells. To do this, you click and drag over all of your data to highlight it. Then use the **Align Center** button on your toolbar (Figure 10-6).

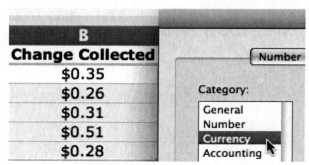

Figure 10-6

9. Next, you are going to change the format of your cells so it displays the correct money unit for the change collected. Click and drag over the numbers in column B to highlight them, go to the **Format** menu and choose **Cells**. Click the **Number** tab, select **Currency**, and click **OK** (Figure 10-7).

Figure 10-7

Money Math Bar Graph *(cont.)*
Activity 10

10. Now you are going to use your data to create a chart. First, highlight all of your data in both columns, including the labels. Choose the **Insert** menu and select **Chart**, then **Bar** (Figure 10-8).

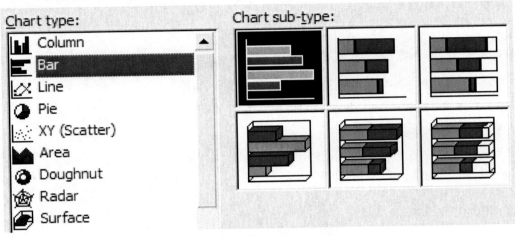

Figure 10-8

11. Click **Next**, and example of your chart should appear. Click the **Next** button again to display the **Chart Options** window. (Figure 10-9).

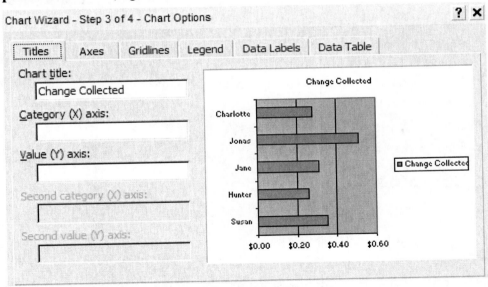

Figure 10-9

12. Click on the **Titles** tab and type "Classroom Change Collected." In the **Category (X) axis** box, type "Student," and in the **Value (Y) axis** box, type "Amount."

13. Click on the **Legend** tab, and remove the checkmark from the **Show Legend** box.

14. Click on the **Data Labels** tab and put a check in the box labeled **Value**.

15. Click **Next** button, check next to **As new sheet**, and click **Finish**. Your chart is now complete!

Multiplication Table
Activity 11

Objectives

Each student will use a spreadsheet program to create a multiplication table.

Benchmarks for Technology Standards

Students will know the characteristics, uses, and basic features of computer software programs, including:

- knowing the common features and uses of spreadsheets
- knowing appropriate software for performing calculations
- using spreadsheet software to add data

Learning Objectives

At the end of this lesson, students will be able to:

1. Create a new spreadsheet document.
2. Know the various terms associated with spreadsheets, including *rows*, *columns*, and *cells*.
3. Utilize the Select All command.
4. Adjust the width of columns within a spreadsheet.
5. Enter data into a spreadsheet.
6. Increase the font size of data within a spreadsheet.
7. Adjust the alignment of data within a cell.
8. Change the style of the font within a spreadsheet.
9. Create a heading for a spreadsheet.

Before the Computer

This activity can be completed using most versions of Microsoft Excel, Open Office, and iWorks.

Variations

Depending on the age and ability level of your students, you may wish to have students change the color and type of font used in the spreadsheet. An example of a completed multiplication table is shown in Figure 11-1.

Multiplication Table *(cont.)*
Activity 11

Multiplication Table

	1	2	3	4	5	6	7	8	9	10
1	1	2	3	4	5	6	7	8	9	10
2	2	4	6	8	10	12	14	16	18	20
3	3	6	9	12	15	18	21	24	27	30
4	4	8	12	16	20	24	28	32	36	40
5	5	10	15	20	25	30	35	40	45	50
6	6	12	18	24	30	36	42	48	54	60
7	7	14	21	28	35	42	49	56	63	70
8	8	16	24	32	40	48	56	64	72	80
9	9	18	27	36	45	54	63	72	81	90
10	10	20	30	40	50	60	70	80	90	100

Figure 11-1

Multiplication Table *(cont.)*
Activity 11

Procedure

1. Open up a new spreadsheet document. Spreadsheets are made up of columns that are identified by letters (A, B, C, etc.) and rows that are identified by numbers (1, 2, 3, etc.).

2. The location within a spreadsheet where a column meets a row is called a cell, and is identified by both a letter and number (Figure 11-2).

Figure 11-2

3. Click into cell **A2**, and type in the number "1." Hit the **enter** key on your keyboard, which will take you down to the next cell below, and type in the number "2." Continue to enter numbers into each cell until you get to the number 10.

4. Next, click into cell **B1** and type in the number "1." Hit the tab key on your keyboard, which will take you over to the next cell, and type "2." Continue to fill in the rest of your numbers until you get to the number 10 (Figure 11-3).

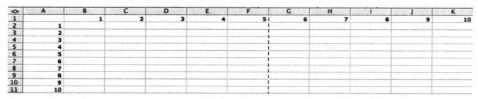

Figure 11-3

5. Hold down the **control** key (or the **command** key on a Mac) and the letter **A** on your keyboard to select all of your cells. Now increase the font size to **18**.

6. With all of your cells selected, use the **Align Center** button to center all of the numbers within your cells.

7. Next, click on the number **1** at the beginning of row 1 to highlight the entire row (Figure 11-4).

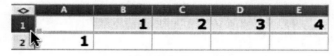

Figure 11-4

Multiplication Table (cont.)
Activity 11

8. Use the **B** button on your toolbar to make the font bold.

9. Now click on the letter **A** at the top of column A to highlight the entire column (Figure 11-5). Make this column bold.

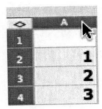

Figure 11-5

10. Hold down the **control** key (**command** on a Mac) and the letter **A** on your keyboard to select all of your cells. Now you are going to reduce the width of your cells. Bring your cursor up to the line between the heading of columns A and B, and click and drag the line to reduce the column width so that the numbers just fit. (Figure 11-6). Continue to do this for each column.

◇	A	B	C	D	E	F
1		**1**	**2**	**3**	**4**	**5**
2	**1**					
3	**2**					

Figure 11-6

11. Next, you will add a title to your spreadsheet. Go to the **View** menu and select **Header and Footer**. Click **Customize Header**... and in the center section, type "Multiplication Table." To view your header, choose the **View** menu and **Page Layout** (Figure 11-7).

Multiplication Table

4	5	6	7	8

Figure 11-7

12. Now that your multiplication table is formatted, you can use your math skills to fill it in. To begin just multiply the numbers in row 1 by the numbers in column A. For example 1 x 1 = 1. Type the number "1" in cell **B2** (Figure 11-8). Continue to fill in your multiplication facts until the table is complete.

	1	**2**	**3**
1	1		
2			

Figure 11-8

Bedtime Column Graph
Activity 12

Objectives

Each student will practice his or her clock-reading skills and enter number data into a spreadsheet to create a simple column graph.

Benchmarks for Technology Standards

Students will know the characteristics, uses, and basic features of computer software programs, including:

- knows the common features and uses of spreadsheets
- uses spreadsheet software to update, add, and delete data, and to produce charts

Learning Objectives

At the end of this lesson, students will be able to:

1. Create a new spreadsheet document.
2. Know the various terms associated with spreadsheets, including *rows*, *columns*, and *cells*.
3. Adjust the width of columns within a spreadsheet.
4. Enter data into a spreadsheet.
5. Adjust the alignment of data within a cell.
6. Change the style of the font within a spreadsheet.
7. Create and format a column chart from data entered within a spreadsheet.

Before the Computer

- This activity can be completed using most versions of Microsoft Excel, Open Office, and iWorks.
- The procedure for formatting charts using spreadsheets may vary depending on the software and version your school uses. Make sure to try the activity with your school's spreadsheet software, and be prepared to modify the chart procedure accordingly.

Variations

Depending on the age and ability level of your students, you may wish to have students collect their own data on the time their classmates last went to bed to create their spreadsheet and chart. An example of a completed column chart is shown in Figure 12-1.

Bedtime Column Graph (cont.)
Activity 12

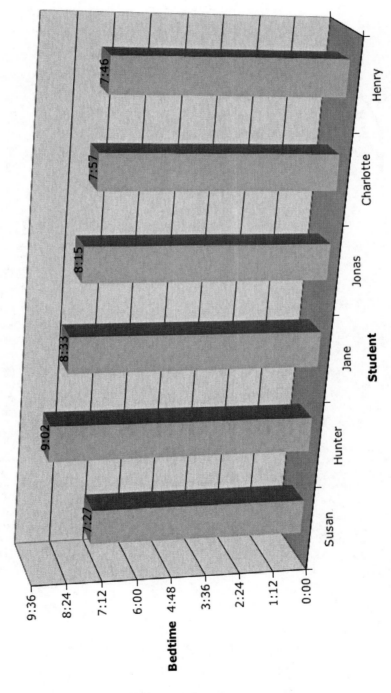

Figure 12-1

Bedtime Column Graph (cont.)
Activity 12

Procedure

1. Begin this activity by recording the time of day each student went to bed the previous night according to the clocks in Figure 12-2.

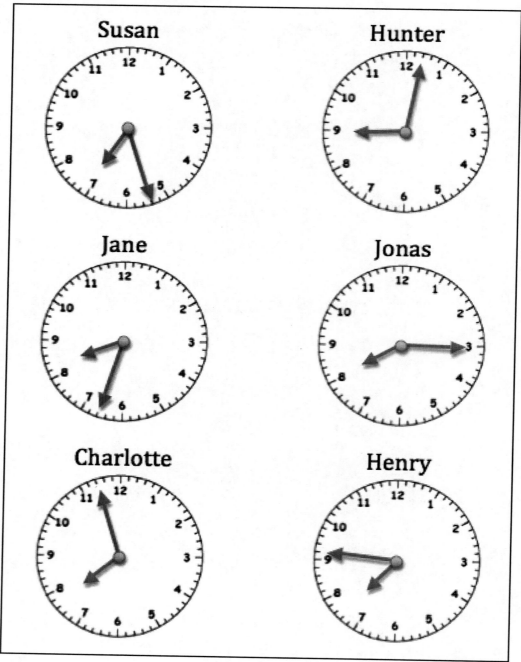

Figure 12-2

Bedtime Column Graph *(cont.)*
Activity 12

2. Open a new spreadsheet document. Spreadsheets are made up of columns that are identified by letters (A, B, C, etc.) and rows that are identified by numbers (1, 2, 3, etc.).

3. The location within a spreadsheet where a column meets a row is called a cell and is identified by both a letter and number (Figure 12-3).

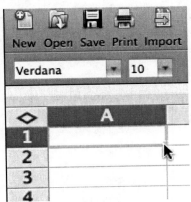

Figure 12-3

4. Click into cell **A1**, and type in the following label: "Student Name." Hit the **enter** key on your keyboard to bring you down to cell **A2**, and type in the name "Susan." Continue to fill in the remaining students' names in Column A.

5. Next click into cell **B1** and type in the following label: "Bedtime." Hit the **enter** key on your keyboard and type in the value for the time each student went to bed.

6. Next, click and drag over the two column labels, and make them bold using the **Bold** button on your toolbar (Figure 12-4).

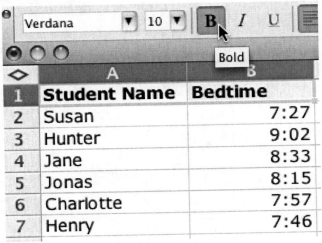

Figure 12-4

Bedtime Column Graph *(cont.)*
Activity 12

7. Now you will center the data in your cells. To do this, you click and drag over all of your data to highlight it. Then use the **Align Center** button on your toolbar (Figure 12-5).

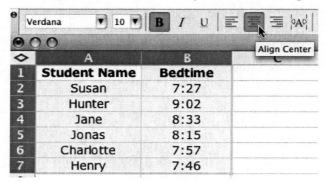

Figure 12-5

8. Now you are going to use your data to create a chart. First, highlight all of your data in both columns, including the labels. Choose the **Insert** menu and select **Chart**, and then choose **Column with a 3-D Visual Effect** (Figure 12-6).

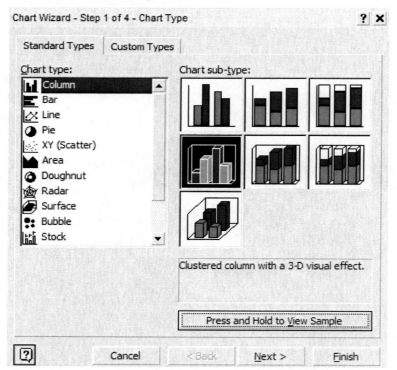

Figure 12-6

9. Click **Next**, and an example of your chart should appear. Click the **Next** button again to display the **Chart Options** window.

Bedtime Column Graph *(cont.)*
Activity 12

10. Click on the **Titles** tab and type in: "What Time Did You Go To Bed?" In the **Category (X) axis** box, type in: "Student," and in the **Value (Z) axis** box, type in: "Bedtime" (Figure 12-7).

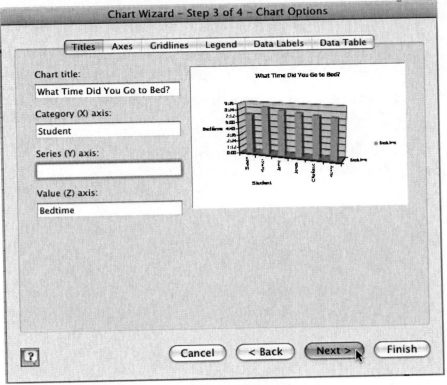

Figure 12-7

11. Click on the **Legend** tab, and remove the checkmark from the **Show Legend** box.

12. Click on the **Data Labels** tab and put a check in the box labeled **Value**.

13. Click the **Next** button, check next to **As new sheet**, and click **Finish** (Figure 12-8).

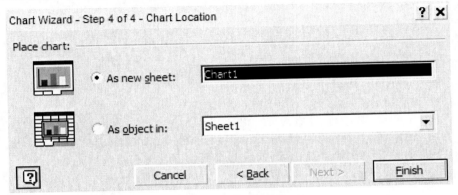

Figure 12-8

14. Your chart is now complete!

Population Explosion Pie Chart
Activity 13

Objectives

Each student will use data on the world's human population to create an area chart using a spreadsheet application.

Benchmarks for Technology Standards

Students will know the characteristics, uses, and basic features of computer software programs, including:

- knowing the common features and uses of spreadsheets
- using spreadsheet software to update, add, and delete data, and to produce charts

Learning Objectives

At the end of this lesson, students will be able to:

1. Create a new spreadsheet document.
2. Know the various terms associated with spreadsheets, including *rows*, *columns*, and *cells*.
3. Adjust the width of columns within a spreadsheet.
4. Enter data into a spreadsheet.
5. Adjust the alignment of data within a cell.
6. Change the style of the font within a spreadsheet.
7. Create and format an exploding pie chart from data entered within a spreadsheet.

Before the Computer

- This activity can be completed using most versions of Microsoft Excel, Open Office, and iWorks.
- The procedure for formatting charts using spreadsheets may vary depending on the software and version your school uses. Make sure to try the activity with your school's spreadsheet software, and be prepared to modify the chart procedure accordingly.

Variations

Depending on the age and ability level of your students, you may wish to have students collect more specific data on world population. For example instead of using continents, you can use geographic regions (Russia, Southeast Asia, India, Middle East, United States, Canada, Europe, etc.) An example of a completed exploded pie chart is shown in Figure 13-1.

Population Explosion Pie Chart *(cont.)*
Activity 13

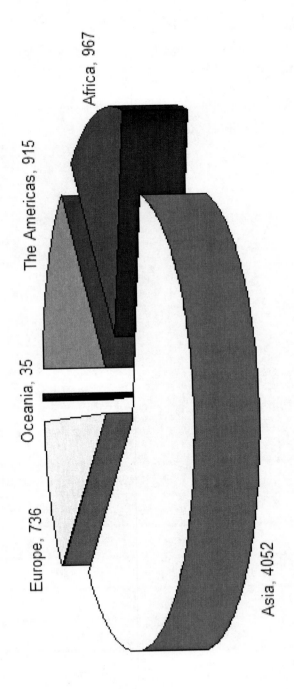

World Population by Region

Africa, 967

The Americas, 915

Oceania, 35

Europe, 736

Asia, 4052

Figure 13-1

Population Explosion Pie Chart *(cont.)*
Activity 13

Procedure

1. Begin this activity by opening a new spreadsheet document. Spreadsheets are made up of columns that are identified by letters (A, B, C, etc.) and rows that are identified by numbers (1, 2, 3, etc.).

2. The location within a spreadsheet where a column meets a row is called a cell, and is identified by both a letter and number (Figure 13-2).

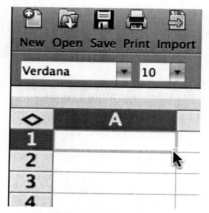

Figure 13-2

3. Click into cell **A1**, and type in the following label: "World Region."

4. Next click into cell **B1** and type in the following label: "Population (Millions)."

5. Now fill in the name of the world region in column **A** and its population in column **B** using the following data.

World Region	Population (Millions)
The Americas	915
Africa	967
Asia	4,052
Europe	736
Oceania	35

6. Next, click and drag over the two column labels, and use the **Bold** button on your toolbar.

7. Now you will center the data in your cells. To do this, click and drag over all of the data, including the labels, to highlight it. Then use the **Align Center** button on your toolbar.

Population Explosion Pie Chart *(cont.)*
Activity 13

8. Next, you will have to widen columns A and B so the label fits within them. To do this take your cursor and place it on the line separating columns A and B. Then click and drag your cursor to the right until the cell is wide enough for the "World Region" label to fit (Figure 13-3).

	A	B	C
1	World Region	Population (Millions)	
2	The Americas	915	
3	Africa	967	
4	Asia	4,052	
5	Europe	736	
6	Oceania	35	

Width: 10.86 (1.13 inches)

Figure 13-3

9. Repeat the same process to widen column B.

10. Now you are going to use your data to create a chart. First, highlight all of your data in both columns, including the labels. Choose the **Insert** menu and select **Chart, Pie**, then **Exploded Pie With a 3-D Visual Effect** (Figure 13-4).

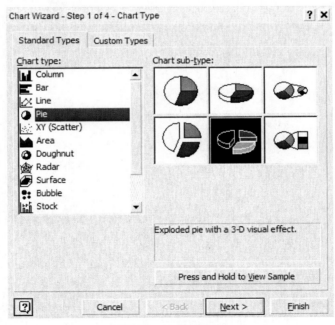

Figure 13-4

11. Click **Next**, and an example of your chart should appear. Click the **Next** button again to display the **Chart Options** window.

12. Click on the **Titles** tab and type "World Population by Region."

13. Click on the **Legend** tab, and remove the checkmark from the **Show Legend** box.

Population Explosion Pie Chart *(cont.)*
Activity 13

14. Click on the **Data Labels** tab and put checkmarks in the boxes labeled **Category Name** and **Value** (Figure 13-5).

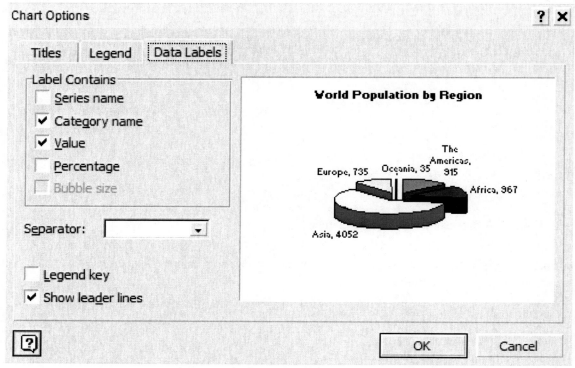

Figure 13-5

15. Click the **Next** button, check next to **As new sheet**, and click **Finish** (Figure 13-6).

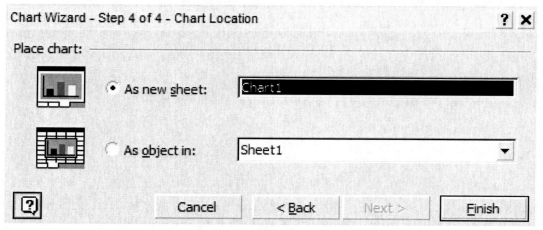

Figure 13-6

16. Your chart is now complete!

Planet Size Bubble Chart
Activity 14

Objectives

Each student will use data on the diameter of the eight planets in the solar system to create a bubble chart, comparing sizes using a spreadsheet application.

Benchmarks for Technology Standards

Students will know the characteristics, uses, and basic features of computer software programs, including:

- knowing the common features and uses of spreadsheets
- using spreadsheet software to update, add, and delete data, and to produce charts

Learning Objectives

At the end of this lesson, students will be able to:

1. Create a new spreadsheet document.
2. Know the various terms associated with spreadsheets, including *rows*, *columns*, and *cells*.
3. Adjust the width of columns within a spreadsheet.
4. Enter data into a spreadsheet.
5. Adjust the alignment of data within a cell.
6. Change the style of the font within a spreadsheet.
7. Copy data from one set of cells and paste it into another column within a spreadsheet.
8. Create and format a 3D bubble chart from data entered within a spreadsheet.

Before the Computer

- This activity can be completed using most versions of Microsoft Excel, Open Office, and iWorks.
- The procedure for formatting charts using spreadsheets may vary depending on the software and version your school uses. Make sure to try the activity with your school's spreadsheet software, and be prepared to modify the chart procedure accordingly.

Variations

Depending on the age and ability level of your students, you may wish to have students change the color of each planet to reflect its true color. An example of a completed 3D bubble chart is shown in Figure 14-1.

Planet Size Bubble Chart (cont.)
Activity 14

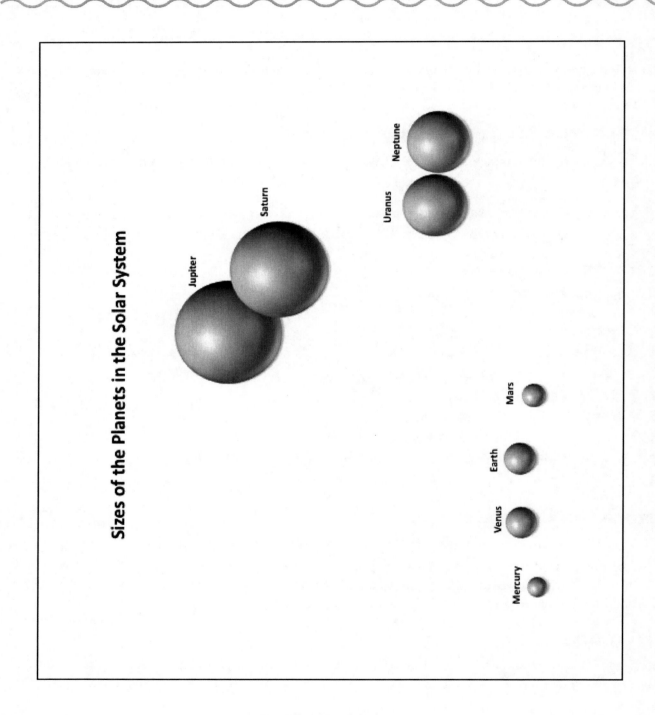

Figure 14-1

Planet Size Bubble Chart *(cont.)*
Activity 14

Procedure

1. Begin this activity by opening a new spreadsheet document. Spreadsheets are made up of columns that are identified by letters (A, B, C, etc.) and rows that are identified by numbers (1, 2, 3, etc.).

2. The location within a spreadsheet where a column meets a row is called a cell, and is identified by both a letter and number (Figure 14-2).

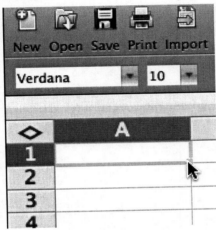

Figure 14-2

3. Click into cell **A1**, and type in the following label: "Planet."

4. Next click into cell **B1** and type in the following label: "Diameter."

5. Now fill in the names of the eight planets within the solar system, along with their diameters, using the following data.

Planet	Diameter
Mercury	4,880
Venus	12,104
Earth	12,756
Mars	6,794
Jupiter	142,984
Saturn	120,536
Uranus	51,118
Neptune	49,532

6. Next, click and drag over the two column labels, and use the **Bold** button on your toolbar.

7. Now you will center your the data in your cells. To do this, you click and drag over all of your data to highlight it. Then use the **Align Center** button on your toolbar.

Planet Size Bubble Chart *(cont.)*
Activity 14

8. In order to create a 3D bubble chart, you must fill in data on the diameter of each planet in column **C**. Instead of retyping it, you can click and drag over the diameter data in column **B** to highlight it, right-click your mouse (or control-click if you are using a Mac), and choose **Copy** (Figure 14-3).

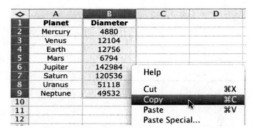

Figure 14-3

9. Now click into cell **C1**, right-click (or control-click) with your mouse, and choose **Paste** (Figure 14-4). Your data should now be in column **C**.

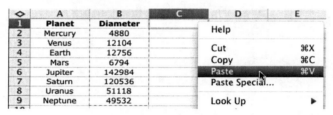

Figure 14-4

10. Now you are going to use your data to create a chart. First, highlight all of your data in all three columns, including the labels. Choose the **Insert** menu, select **Chart**, and choose **Bubble 3-D Visual Effect** (Figure 14-5).

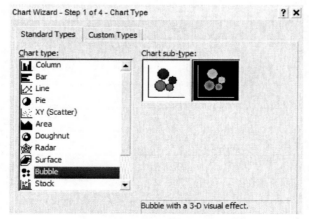

Figure 14-5

12. Click **Next**, and an example of your chart should appear. Click the **Next** button again to display the **Chart Options** window.

13. Click on the **Titles** tab and type "Sizes of the Planets in the Solar System."

Planet Size Bubble Chart *(cont.)*
Activity 14

14. Click on the **Axes** tab and remove the checkmarks from the boxes next to **Value (X) axis**, and **Value (Y) axis**.

15. Click on the **Gridlines** tab and remove the checkmark from **Gridlines** (Figure 14-6).

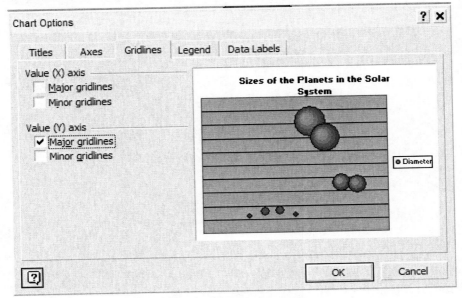

Figure 14-6

16. Click on the **Legend** tab, and remove the checkmark from the **Show Legend** box.

17. Click on the **Data Labels** tab and put a checkmark in the box labeled **X Value**.

18. Click **Next** button, check next to **As new sheet**, and click **Finish** (Figure 14-7).

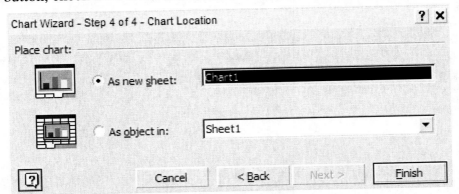

Figure 14-7

19. Your chart is now complete!

Favorite Doughnut Chart
Activity 15

Objectives

Each student will use data collected about his or her classmates' favorite doughnuts to create a doughnut chart which uses a spreadsheet application.

Benchmarks for Technology Standards

Students will know the characteristics, uses, and basic features of computer software programs, including:

- knowing the common features and uses of spreadsheets
- using spreadsheet software to update, add, and delete data, and to produce charts

Learning Objectives

At the end of this lesson, students will be able to:

1. Create a new spreadsheet document.
2. Know the various terms associated with spreadsheets, including *rows*, *columns*, and *cells*.
3. Adjust the width of columns within a spreadsheet.
4. Enter data into a spreadsheet.
5. Adjust the alignment of data within a cell.
6. Change the style of the font within a spreadsheet.
7. Create and format a doughnut chart from data entered within a spreadsheet.

Before the Computer

- This activity can be completed using most versions of Microsoft Excel, Open Office, and iWorks.
- The procedure for formatting charts using spreadsheets may vary depending on the software and version your school uses. Make sure to try the activity with your school's spreadsheet software, and be prepared to modify the chart procedure accordingly.

Variations

Example data from a fictitious class is used in this activity. You may wish to have students collect their own data on their classmates' favorite doughnuts by tallying them. Depending on the age and ability level of your students, you may also choose to tally other favorite foods as well. An example of a completed doughnut chart is shown in Figure 15-1.

Favorite Doughnut Chart (cont.)
Activity 15

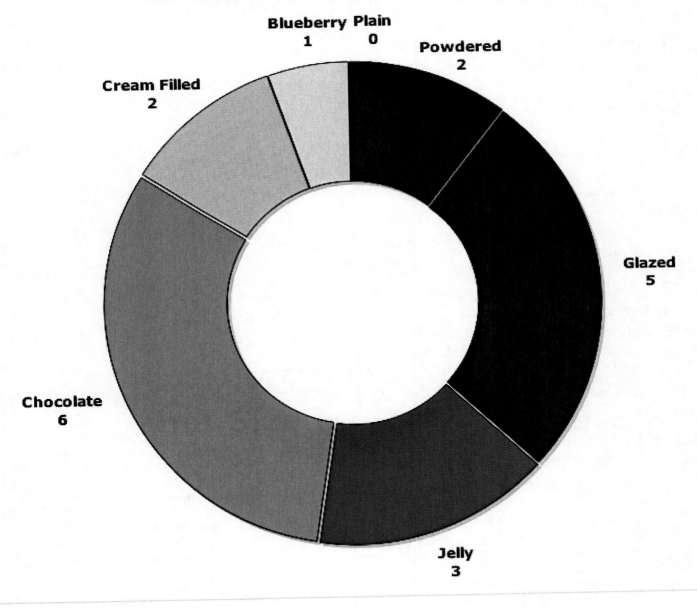

Our Class's Favorite Doughnuts

Blueberry 1
Plain 0
Powdered 2
Glazed 5
Jelly 3
Chocolate 6
Cream Filled 2

Figure 15-1

Favorite Doughnut Chart *(cont.)*
Activity 15

Procedure

1. Begin this activity by opening a new spreadsheet document. Spreadsheets are made up of columns that are identified by letters (A, B, C, etc.) and rows that are identified by numbers (1, 2, 3, etc.).

2. The location within a spreadsheet where a column meets a row is called a cell, and is identified by both a letter and number (Figure 15-2).

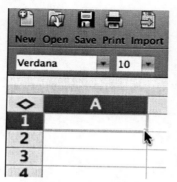

Figure 15-2

3. Click into cell **A1**, and type in the following label: "Favorite Doughnut."

4. Next click into cell **B1** and type in the following label: "Number of Students."

5. Now use the following data to fill in the names of the types of doughnuts in column A, and the number of students who liked them in column B.

Favorite Doughnut	Number of Students
Plain	0
Powdered	2
Glazed	5
Jelly	3
Chocolate	6
Cream Filled	2
Blueberry	1

6. Next, click and drag over the two column labels, and use the **Bold** button on your toolbar.

7. Now you will center the data in your cells. To do this, click and drag over all of the data to highlight it. Then use the **Align Center** button on your toolbar.

Favorite Doughnut Chart *(cont.)*
Activity 15

8. Next, you will have to widen columns **A** and **B** so the label fits within them. To do this, take your cursor and place it on the line separating columns A and B. Then click and drag your cursor to the right until the cell is wide enough for the "Favorite Doughnut" label to fit in (Figure 15-3).

	A	B	C
	Favorite Doughnut	**ber of Students**	
1			
2	Plain	0	
3	Powdered	2	
4	Glazed	5	
5	Jelly	3	
6	Chocolate	6	
7	Cream Filled	2	
8	Blueberry	1	

Width: 16.57 (1.68 inches)

Figure 15-3

9. Repeat the same process to widen column **B** so you can read the "Number of Students" label.

10. Now you are going to use your data to create a chart. First, highlight all of your data in both columns, including the labels. Choose the **Insert** menu and select **Chart**, then choose **Doughnut** (Figure 15-4).

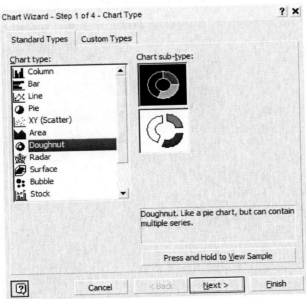

Figure 15-4

11. Click **Next**, and an example of your chart should appear. Click the **Next** button again to display the **Chart Options** window.

12. Click on the **Titles** tab and type "Our Class's Favorite Doughnuts."

Favorite Doughnut Chart *(cont.)*
Activity 15

13. Click on the **Legend** tab, and remove the checkmark from the **Show Legend** box.

14. Click on the **Data Labels** tab and put checkmarks in the boxes labeled **Category Name** and **Value**. Then click the small arrow next to **Separator** and choose **New Line** (Figure 15-5). (If you are using Excel 2007 or 2008, you may not see these options. Click on **Show Label** only.)

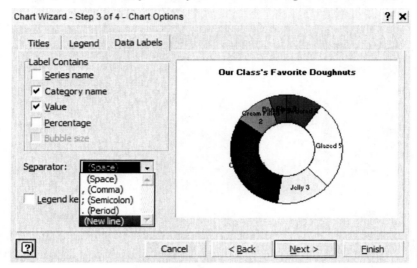

Figure 15-5

15. Click the **Next** button, check next to **As new sheet**, and click **Finish** (Figure 13-6).

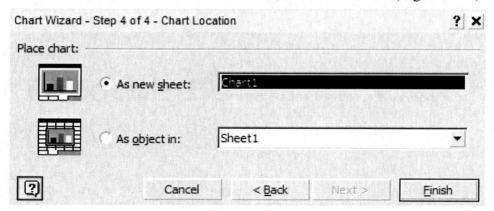

Figure 15-6

16. Your chart is now complete!

Daily Temperature Line Chart
Activity 16

Objectives

Each student will use local weather data to create a line chart showing the daily tenperature over a five-day period at his or her school.

Benchmarks for Technology Standards

Students will know the characteristics, uses, and basic features of computer software programs, including:

- knowing the common features and uses of spreadsheets
- using spreadsheet software to update, add, and delete data, and to produce charts

Learning Objectives

At the end of this lesson, students will be able to:

1. Create a new spreadsheet document.
2. Know the various terms associated with spreadsheets, including *rows*, *columns*, and *cells*.
3. Adjust the width of columns within a spreadsheet.
4. Enter data into a spreadsheet.
5. Adjust the alignment of data within a cell.
6. Change the style of the font within a spreadsheet.
7. Format the date within a spreadsheet.
8. Create and format a line chart from data entered within a spreadsheet.

Before the Computer

- This activity can be completed using most versions of Microsoft Excel, Open Office, and iWorks.
- The procedure for formatting charts using spreadsheets may vary depending on the software and version your school uses. Make sure to try the activity with your school's spreadsheet software, and be prepared to modify the chart procedure accordingly.

Variations

Depending on the age and ability level of your students, you may wish to have them make a line graph for other weather variables like humidity and pressure. An example of a completed line chart is shown in Figure 16-1.

Daily Temperature Line Chart (cont.)
Activity 16

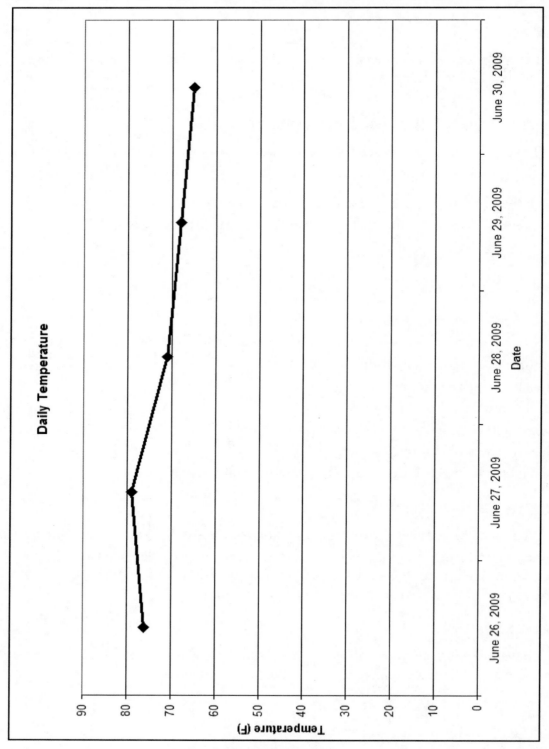

Figure 16-1

Daily Temperature Line Chart *(cont.)*
Activity 16

Procedure

1. Open a new spreadsheet document. Spreadsheets are made up of columns that are identified by letters (A, B, C, etc.) and rows that are identified by numbers (1, 2, 3, etc.).

2. The location within a spreadsheet where a column meets a row is called a cell, and is identified by both a letter and number (Figure 16-2).

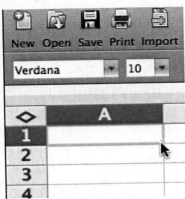

Figure 16-2

3. Click into cell **A1**, and type in the following label: "Date." Hit the **tab** key on your keyboard to bring you over to cell **B1**, and type in the label "Temperature (Degrees F)."

4. Next, click and drag over the two column labels, and use the **Bold** button on your toolbar.

5. Next, you will have to widen columns **A** and **B** so the label fits within them. To do this take your cursor and place it in between the line separating columns **B** and **C**. Then click and drag your cursor to the right until the cell is wide enough for the "Temperature (Degrees F)" label to fit in (Figure 16-3).

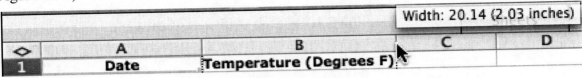

Figure 16-3

6. Now fill in the following data on date and temperature into your spreadsheet.

Date	Temperature (Degrees F)
June 26, 2009	76
June 27, 2009	79
June 28, 2009	71
June 29, 2009	68
June 30, 2009	65

Daily Temperature Line Chart *(cont.)*
Activity 16

7. Now you will center your the data in your cells. To do this, click and drag over all of your data to highlight it. Then use the **Align Center** button on your toolbar.

8. Next, you will change the format of the dates within column A. To do this, click and drag over the dates in column **A**, choose the **Format** menu, and select **Cells**. Select **Number**, and choose the date format that displays the year (Figure 16-4).

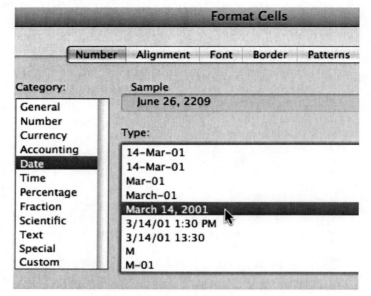

Figure 16-4

9. Now you are going to use your data to create a chart. First, highlight all of your data in both columns, including the labels. Choose the **Insert** menu, select **Chart**, and choose **Line** (Figure 16-5).

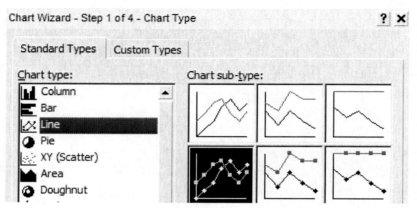

Figure 16-5

10. Click **Next**, and an example of your chart should appear. Click the **Next** button again to display the **Chart Options** window.

Daily Temperature Line Chart *(cont.)*
Activity 16

11. Click on the **Titles** tab and type in: "Daily Temperature." In the **Category (X)** axis box, type "Date" and in **the Value (Y) axis** box, type "Temperature (F)."

12. Click on the **Axes** tab and select **Category** under **Category (X) axis** (Figure 16-6).

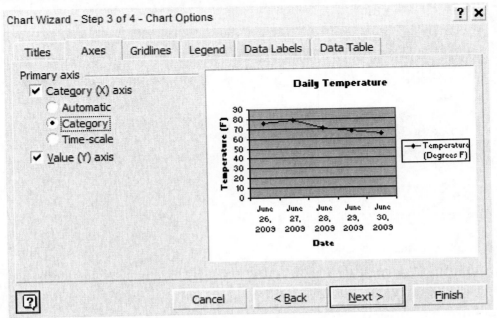

Figure 16-6

13. Click on the **Legend** tab, and remove the checkmark from the **Show Legend** box.

14. Click the **Next** button, check next to **As new sheet**, and click **Finish** (Figure 16-7).

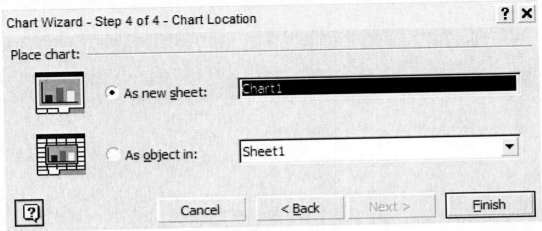

Figure 16-7

15. Your chart is now complete!

Mountain Surface Chart
Activity 17

Objectives

Each student will enter elevation data into a spreadsheet and then use it to create a three-dimensional surface chart representing the top of a mountain.

Benchmarks for Technology Standards

Students will know the characteristics, uses, and basic features of computer software programs, including:

- knowing the common features and uses of spreadsheets
- using spreadsheet software to update, add, and delete data, and to produce charts

Learning Objectives

At the end of this lesson, students will be able to:

1. Create a new spreadsheet document.
2. Know the various terms associated with spreadsheets, including *rows*, *columns*, and *cells*.
3. Adjust the width of columns within a spreadsheet.
4. Enter data into a spreadsheet.
5. Adjust the alignment of data within a cell.
6. Change the style of the font within a spreadsheet.
7. Create and format a 3D surface chart from data entered within a spreadsheet.
8. Change the background color of a chart.

Before the Computer

- This activity can be completed using most versions of Microsoft Excel, Open Office, and iWorks.
- The procedure for formatting charts using spreadsheets may vary depending on the software and version your school uses. Make sure to try the activity with your school's spreadsheet software, and be prepared to modify the chart procedure accordingly.

Variations

Depending on the age and ability level of your students, you may wish to have students experiment with changing the 3D view of the chart. They can do this by right-clicking (or control-clicking) on the background of the chart and choosing **3D View**. An example of a completed column chart is shown in Figure 17-1.

Mountain Surface Chart (cont.)
Activity 17

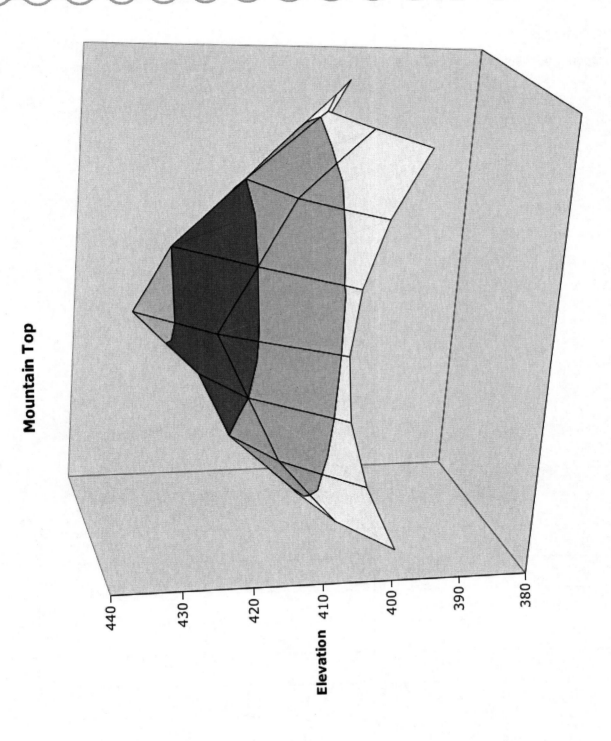

Figure 17-1

Mountain Surface Chart *(cont.)*
Activity 17

Procedure

1. Open a new spreadsheet document. Spreadsheets are made up of columns that are identified by letters (A, B, C, etc.) and rows that are identified by numbers (1, 2, 3, etc.).

2. The location within a spreadsheet where a column meets a row is called a cell, and is identified by both a letter and number (Figure 17-2).

Figure 17-2

3. Click into cell **A1**, and type in the following label: "Elevation 1." Hit the **tab** key on your keyboard to bring you over to cell **B1**, and type in the label "Elevation 2." Continue to create headings for columns C, D, and E (Figure 17-3).

	A	B	C	D	E
1	Elevation 1	Elevation 2	Elevation 3	Elevation 4	Elevation 5
2					
3					

Figure 17-3

4. Next, click and drag over the two column labels, and use the **Bold** button on your toolbar.

5. Now fill the following elevation data into your spreadsheet.

Elevation 1	Elevation 2	Elevation 3	Elevation 4	Elevation 5
400	406	409	406	400
405	415	420	415	405
408	420	425	420	408
409	425	435	425	409
408	420	430	420	408
405	415	420	415	405
400	405	409	405	400

6. Next you will center the data in your cells. To do this, click and drag over all of your data to highlight it. Then use the **Align Center** button on your toolbar.

Mountain Surface Chart (cont.)
Activity 17

7. Now you are going to use your data to create a chart. First, highlight all of your data in the columns, including the labels. Choose the **Insert** menu, select **Chart**, then choose **Surface**, and **3-D Surface**. (Figure 17-4).

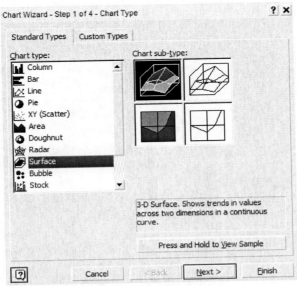

Figure 17-4

8. Click **Next**, and an example of your chart should appear. Click the **Next** button again to display the **Chart Options** window.

9. Click on the **Titles** tab and type "Mountain Top." In the **Value (Z) axis** box, type "Elevation."

10. Click on the **Axes** tab and remove the checkmarks from **Category (X) axis** and **Series (Y) axis**.

11. Click on the **Gridlines** tab, and remove the checkmark from the **Value (Z) axis Major Gridlines** box.

12. Click on the **Legend** tab, and remove the checkmark from the **Show Legend** box.

13. Click the **Next** button, check next to **As new sheet**, and click **Finish**. Or go to the **Chart** menu, choose **Move Chart**, and save **As a New Sheet** (Figure 17-5).

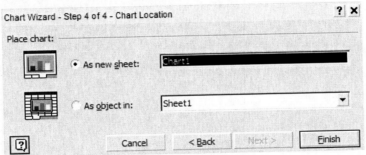

Figure 17-5

Mountain Surface Chart *(cont.)*
Activity 17

14. Next, you are going to change the background color of your chart. Double-click on the background to bring up the **Format** window. Choose **Fill** or **Area**, and select a color for your background (Figure 17-6). Then click **OK**.

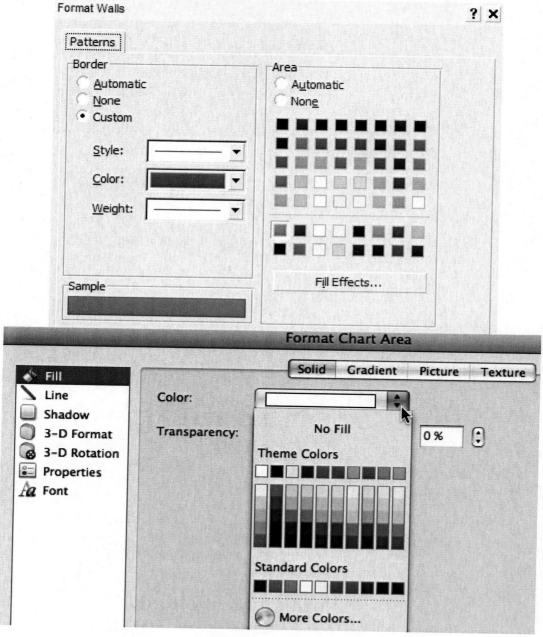

Figure 17-6

15. Your chart is now complete!

Fraction Charts
Activity 18

Objectives

Each student will enter data into a spreadsheet to create pie charts representing four different types of fractions.

Benchmarks for Technology Standards

Students will know the characteristics, uses, and basic features of computer software programs, including:

- knowing the common features and uses of spreadsheets
- using spreadsheet software to update, add, and delete data, and to produce charts

Learning Objectives

At the end of this lesson, students will be able to:

1. Create a new spreadsheet document.
2. Know the various terms associated with spreadsheets, including *rows*, *columns*, and *cells*.
3. Enter data into a spreadsheet.
4. Adjust the alignment of data within a cell.
5. Change the style of the font within a spreadsheet.
6. Change the format of a number within a cell.
7. Create and format multiple pie charts from data entered within a spreadsheet.
8. Change the background color of a chart.

Before the Computer

- This activity can be completed using most versions of Microsoft Excel, Open Office, and iWorks.
- The procedure for formatting charts using spreadsheets may vary depending on the software and version your school uses. Make sure to try the activity with your school's spreadsheet software, and be prepared to modify the chart procedure accordingly.

Variations

Depending on the age and ability level of your students, you may wish to have students create other types of fraction examples, using sixths, sixteenths, etc. An example of the completed pie chart is shown in Figure 18-1.

Fraction Charts (cont.)
Activity 18

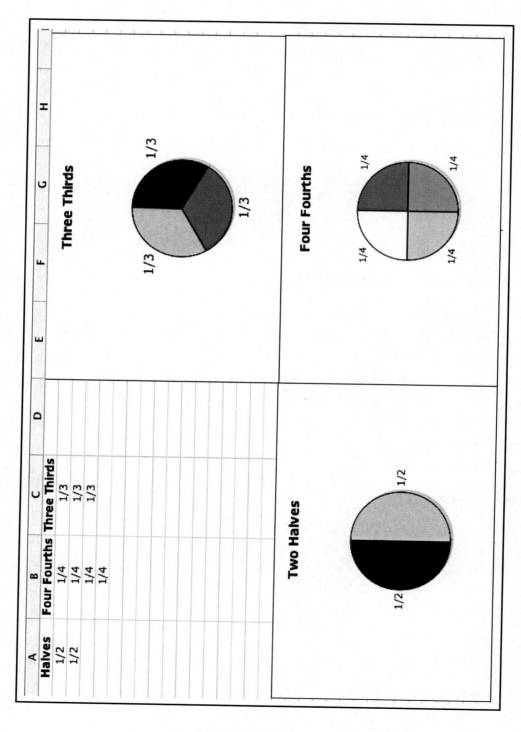

Figure 18-1

84

Fraction Charts *(cont.)*
Activity 18

Procedure

1. Open a new spreadsheet document. Spreadsheets are made up of columns that are identified by letters (A, B, C, etc.) and rows that are identified by numbers (1, 2, 3, etc.).

2. The location within a spreadsheet where a column meets a row is called a cell, and is identified by both a letter and number (Figure 18-2).

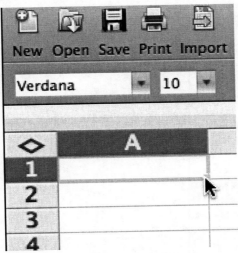

Figure 18-2

3. Click into cell **A1**, and type the following label: "Halves." Hit the **enter** key on your keyboard to bring you down to cell **A2**, and type in "0.5." Repeat this for cell **A3** also (Figure 18-3).

◇	A	B
1	**Halves**	
2	0.5	
3	0.5	
4		

Figure 18-3

4. Next, click and drag over your data, and use the **Align Center** button on your toolbar. Then select the label and use the **Bold** button to make it bold (Figure 18-4).

Figure 18-4

Fraction Charts *(cont.)*
Activity 18

5. Now you are going to change the format of the numbers within your column to display them as fractions. Click and drag over only the numbers in column **A** to highlight them, choose the **Format** menu, and **Cells**. Click the **Number** tab, select **Fraction**, then **Up To One Digit**, and hit **OK** (Figure 18-5).

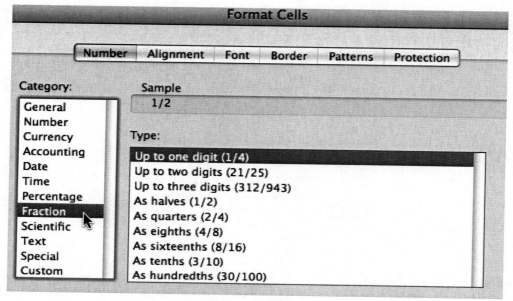

Figure 18-5

6. Now you are going to use your data to create a chart. First, highlight all of your data by clicking and dragging over it. Choose the **Insert** menu, select **Chart**, and then choose **Pie**.

7. Click **Next**, and an example of your chart should appear. Click the **Next** button again to display the **Chart Options** window.

8. Click on the **Titles** tab and type "Two Halves."

9. Click on the **Legend** tab, and remove the checkmark from the **Show Legend** box.

10. Click on the **Data Labels** tab, and put a checkmark in the **Show Value** box, or double-click on your chart, choose **Labels**, and then **Value** (Figure 18-6).

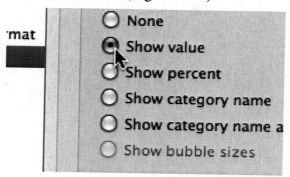

Figure 18-6

Fraction Charts *(cont.)*
Activity 18

11. Click the **Next** button, check next to **As object in**, and click **Finish**. Or go to the **Chart** menu, choose **Move Chart**, and save as an **Object** (Figure 18-7).

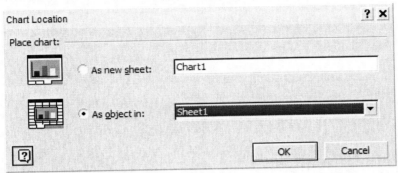

Figure 18-7

12. Next, you are going to resize your chart. To do this, click on the anchor point on the upper-right corner of the chart, and drag it down toward the bottom-left corner until it is about half its original size (Figure 18-8).

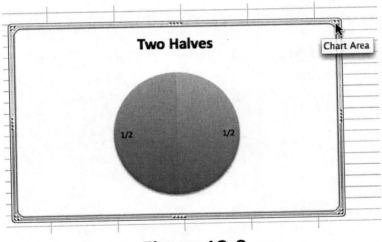

Figure 18-8

13. Now click and drag your chart to lower-left part of your spreadsheet.

14. Next you are going to create a chart showing quarter fractions. Click into cell **B1**, type in the label "Four Fourths," and then fill in the data shown in Figure 18-9.

B
Four Fourths
0.25
0.25
0.25
0.25

Figure 18-9

Fraction Charts *(cont.)*
Activity 18

15. Change the format of the numbers within your column to display as fractions. Click and drag over only the numbers in column **B** to highlight them, choose the **Format** menu, and **Cells**. Click the **Number** tab, select **Fraction, Up To One Digit**, and hit **OK**.

16. Highlight all the data in column **B** and make another pie chart, formatting it just like the first one. Make sure to save it **As object in**. Reduce its size and drag it next to your first pie chart (Figure 18-10).

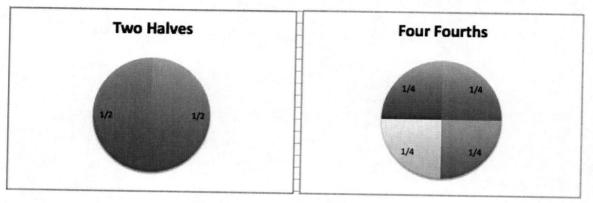

Figure 18-10

17. Next, click into cell **C1**, and type in the following label: "Three Thirds."

18. Make the label bold and center it within the cell using the buttons on your toolbar.

19. Fill in the data shown in Figure 18-11 in the cells below your label.

C
Three Thirds
0.33
0.33
0.33

Figure 18-11

20 Highlight all of the numbers in column **C**, and format them as fractions using the **Format** menu, choosing **Cells**, and then **Fraction**.

21. Select all the data in column **C** to create your third pie chart. Format it the same as your previous two charts.

22. Your charts are now complete, and should appear like the ones in Figure 18-1.

Tree ID Pyramid Chart
Activity 19

Objectives

Each student will enter data on a survey of conifer trees to create a three-dimensional pyramid chart.

Benchmarks for Technology Standards

Students will know the characteristics, uses, and basic features of computer software programs, including:

- knowing the common features and uses of spreadsheets
- using spreadsheet software to update, add, and delete data, and to produce charts

Learning Objectives

At the end of this lesson, students will be able to:

1. Create a new spreadsheet document.
2. Know the various terms associated with spreadsheets, including *rows*, *columns*, and *cells*.
3. Enter data into a spreadsheet.
4. Adjust the alignment of data within a cell.
5. Change the style of the font within a spreadsheet.
6. Create and format a cone chart from data entered within a spreadsheet.
7. Change the color of the data displayed within a chart.
8. Change the background color of a chart.

Before the Computer

- This activity can be completed using most versions of Microsoft Excel, Open Office, and iWorks.
- The procedure for formatting charts using spreadsheets may vary depending on the software and version your school uses. Make sure to try the activity with your school's spreadsheet software, and be prepared to modify the chart procedure accordingly.

Variations

Depending on the age and ability level of your students, you may wish to have students conduct their own survey of trees around the school, their homes, or a nearby park to create their spreadsheet and cone chart. An example of a completed pyramid chart is shown in Figure 19-1.

Tree ID Pyramid Chart *(cont.)*
Activity 19

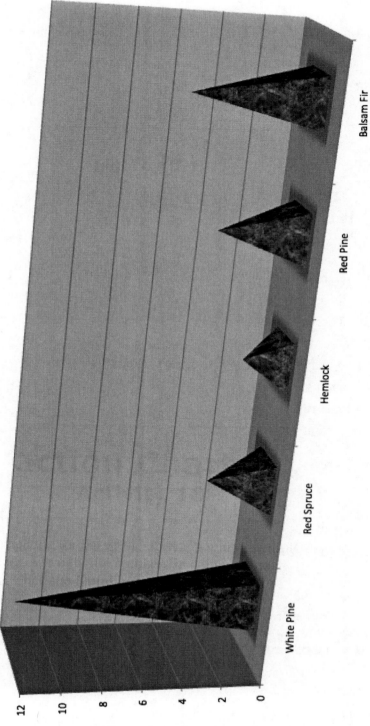

Figure 19-1

Tree ID Pyramid Chart *(cont.)*
Activity 19

Procedure

1. Open a new spreadsheet document. Spreadsheets are made up of columns that are identified by letters (A, B, C, etc.) and rows that are identified by numbers (1, 2, 3, etc.).

2. The location within a spreadsheet where a column meets a row is called a cell, and is identified by both a letter and number (Figure 19-2).

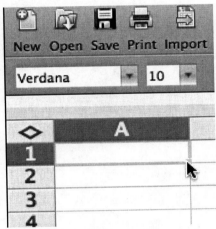

Figure 19-2

3. Click into cell **A1**, and type "Tree Species" for the column label. Hit the **tab** key on your keyboard to bring you over to cell **B1**. Type in "Amount" as the label.

4. Fill the data into the correct cells of your spreadsheet using the following data.

Tree Species	Amount
White Pine	12
Red Spruce	3
Hemlock	2
Red Pine	4
Balsam Fir	6

5. Next, click and drag over the two column labels, and use the **Bold** and **Align Center** buttons on your toolbar (Figure 19-3).

Figure 19-3

Tree ID Pyramid Chart *(cont.)*
Activity 19

6. Now you are going to use your data to create a chart. With all of your data still highlighted, choose the **Insert** menu and select **Chart**, and then **Pyramid**, or choose **Column** and **3-D Pyramid** (Figure 19-4).

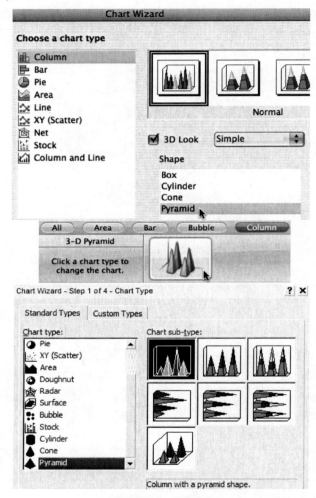

Figure 19-4

7. Click **Next**, and an example of your chart should appear. Click the **Next** button again to display the **Chart Options** window.

8. Click on the **Titles** tab and type "Conifer Tree Survey." In the **Category (X) axis** box, type "Tree Species," and in the **Value (Z) axis box**, type "Amount."

9. Click on the **Legend** tab, and remove the checkmark from the **Show Legend** box.

10. Click on the **Data Labels** tab and put a check in the box labeled **Value**.

11. Click the **Next** button, check next to **As New Sheet**, and click **Finish**, or go to the **Chart** menu and choose **Move Chart**, and then select **As New Sheet**.

Tree ID Pyramid Chart *(cont.)*
Activity 19

12. Now you will change the color of the pyramids within your chart. Double-click on one of the pyramids to bring up the **Format Data Series** window. If you are using Excel, click the **Patterns** tab, and choose **Fill Effects** or **Fill**. Select **Texture** and choose **Green Marble**, then click **OK** (Figure 19-5). If you are using **Open Office**, click the **Area** tab and select **Bitmap**, then choose **Leaves** and click **OK** (Figure 19-6).

Figure 19-5

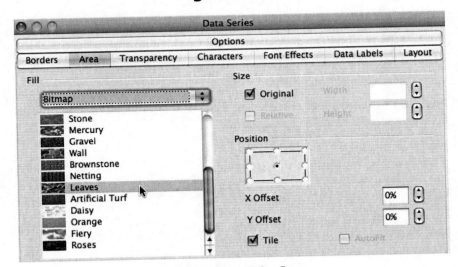

Figure 19-6

13. Next you are going to change the background color of your chart. To do this, double-click on the background and change the **Area color** to a very light blue. Click **OK**, and your chart is complete!

Presentation Software Tutorial
Activity 20

Objectives

Each student will become familiar with how to use presentation software to create a simple presentation.

Benchmarks for Technology Standards

Students will know the characteristics, uses, and basic features of computer software programs, including:

knowing the common features and uses of desktop publishing software (e.g., documents are created, designed, and formatted for publication; data and graphics can be imported into a document using desktop software)

Learning Objectives

At the end of this lesson, students will be able to:

1. Create a new presentation document.
2. Know the various terms associated with presentations, including *slides*, *theme*, *slide show*, *normal view*, *title*, and *subtitle*.
3. Select a theme for a presentation.
4. Insert a title into a presentation.
5. Insert a subtitle into a presentation.
6. Insert an image into a presentation.
7. Change the size of the font within a presentation.
8. Create a new slide within a presentation.
9. View the presentation as a slide show.

Before the Computer

- This activity can be completed using most presentation software, including PowerPoint, Open Office, and Keynote.
- The procedure for formatting charts using spreadsheets may vary depending on the software and version your school uses. Make sure to try the activity with your school's spreadsheet software, and be prepared to modify the chart procedure accordingly.

Variations

Depending on the age and ability level of your students, you may wish to have students create a presentation on a favorite author, animal, etc. A presentation about a pine tree is provided as an example of how to create a presentation.

Presentation Software Tutorial *(cont.)*
Activity 20

Procedure

1. Begin this activity by opening a new presentation. In this activity you will create a slide show about pine trees.

2. First you will choose a theme for your presentation. A theme is a specific set of colors and font styles for your presentation. Go to the **Format** menu and select **Slide Theme** to bring up the theme gallery (Figure 20-1). Choose a theme that you like.

Figure 20-1

3. The first slide will appear. Click into the text box that reads **Click To Add Title.** Type the following title: "White Pine Trees."

4. In the **Click to Add Subtitles** box, type in: "by (Your Name)."

5. Go to the **Insert** menu and choose **New Slide.** This will inset a new slide into your presentation. Click into the **Click to Add Title** box and type "All About Pine Trees."

6. Next, click into the **Click to Add Text box.** Type in the following fact about pine trees: "Height: 80 to 100 feet." Hit the **enter** key on your keyboard to automatically insert another bullet in your list. Continue to add the following facts about pine trees:

- Long Green Needles
- Five Needles Per Group
- Smooth Gray/Green Bark
- Narrow Cones
- Live 100–450 Years
- Like Moist Soil
- Used for Lumber

Presentation Software Tutorial *(cont.)*
Activity 20

7. Insert a new slide. Go to the **Format** menu, choose **Slide Layout**, and select **Picture With Caption**. Notice that on the left side of your screen, each slide is listed in the slide sorter. This allows you to quickly select a slide to work on (Figure 20-2).

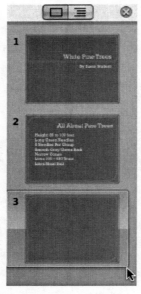

Figure 20-2

8. Next, open up your web browser and have your teacher help you locate an image of a pine tree. Once you locate one, right-click on it (or control-click if you are using a Mac), and choose **Copy**. Return to your blank slide, right-click (or control-click) on it, and select **Paste**. Your image should now appear in your slide. Resize the image by clicking and dragging on one of the corner anchor points.

9. Now click into the **Click To Add Title** box, and type "White Pine Tree."

10. Next click into the **Click To Add Text box** and type "Image Source:" followed by the name of the website from which you copied your image.

11. Your presentation is now complete! To view it as a slide show, click on the title slide in the **Slide Sort** window. Then click on the **Slide Show** button (Figure 20-3). Click your mouse to advance to your next slide.

Figure 20-3